ETS® Pathwise®

Data-Driven
School Improvement Series

CREATING A DATA-DRIVEN SYSTEM

Peter J. Holly

Educational Testing Service
MS 18-D
Rosedale Road
Princeton, NJ 08541-0001
Web site: http://www.ets.org/pathwise

ISBN 0-88685-247-1

Printed in the United States of America

07 06 05 04 03 02 10 9 8 7 6 5 4 3 2 1

Table of Contents

PREFACE

This is the fifth workbook in the PATHWISE® *Data-Driven School Improvement Series*. Whereas Workbook Four: *Analyzing and Understanding Data* explores the importance of scientifically-based research and its strategic relationship with school-based research in the implementation of the *No Child Left Behind* legislation, Workbook Five: *Creating a Data-Driven System* goes one stage further. Building on pathfinding work in school systems across the nation, the author provides a model of what can be done to become a **data-using system** at the local level. In building on current practice, this model also extrapolates from the present to the future tense by fitting the existing puzzle pieces into a more holistic, comprehensive system of data-use.

According to Denis Doyle (2002):

> **As the 21st Century unfolds, two intertwined terms are becoming, if not household words, schoolhouse phrases: "data-driven decision making" and "scientifically based research." Both are a part of the No Child Left Behind Act, but they are not important because NCLB includes them. The federal act includes them because they are important.**

That is a vital point. These terms are included in the federal legislation because of their importance. Indeed, continues Doyle:

> **Data-driven decision making is the foundational activity that underlies the No Child Left Behind Act of 2001. Signed into law on Jan. 8, 2002, the act is genuinely historic....Six months into NCLB schools are now required by law to use data. They must use data to change organizational and individual behavior and they must use data to change academic outcomes.**

The challenge, then, is for local educators across the nation to systematize their use of data-based decision making for the twin purposes of accountability and development.

In adopting a systems approach to examining the importance of data-based decision making at the local level, this workbook has two potential audiences. The first audience is all of us who work in the education field today. We are all fast becoming providers and users of data to inform our decision making at various levels of the educational system. Indeed, in the kind of school system envisioned in this workbook, everyone is a data user in order to make informed decisions at every operational level. The kind of administrator described by Ezarik (2002) as "data man" will become the rarity as no one person will be over-identified with data and its use. However, the kind of enthusiasm, commitment, and curiosity demonstrated by this same administrator ("With the data in front of me, I need to start digging in. I need to know the 'why' of the problem!") will become much more commonplace and percolate throughout the organization. We will all be data men and data women.

In addition, some support people will be required to service, facilitate, and coordinate the data-using process. The second audience for this workbook, therefore, is more specific—those educators with responsibility for preparing the ground, organizing, and providing the wherewithal for data-based decision making in schools and school districts. Killion and Bellamy (2000), for instance, have described the role of the school-based data analyst. Such an educator, they say, supports school improvement by collecting, organizing, analyzing, and displaying data about student achievement and school factors associated with achievement. But the role is very much a service one so that other people can then use the organized, analyzed, and displayed data to make their informed decisions. According to Killion and Bellamy, it is the capacity for data use that has to be diffused throughout the local school system. It is data use that has to become job-embedded.

> Understanding and using data about school and student performance are fundamental to improving schools. Without analyzing and discussing data, schools are unlikely to identify and solve the problems that need attention, identify appropriate interventions to solve those problems, or know how they are progressing toward achievement of their goals. Data are the fuel of reform....Because data abound, schools must become data savvy. Everyone needs to understand what information is available about the school and its students and what data are relevant to the school's immediate needs. Committees need to review data related to decisions and actions they are considering. Data collection needs to be planned to guide formative and summative evaluation of programs and projects. Ongoing analysis of data provides insights into mid-course changes necessary to reach established goals....In short, using data separates good schools from mediocre schools. Schools that are increasing student achievement, staff productivity and collegiality, and customer satisfaction use data to inform and guide their decisions and actions. Data use essentially sets a course of action and keeps a staff on that course to school improvement and student success (Killion and Bellamy, 2000).

This dispersal of data use throughout the local system can be enhanced, however, by the work of a school-based data analyst. Such an educator, say Killion and Bellamy (2000), should

- be a teacher and not an administrator (thus increasing access to and interest in data by other teacher colleagues)
- be a member of the school's leadership team
- provide support to student-focused action teams—school action research teams that are responsible for developing and testing interventions to achieve school improvement goals

- organize information about the school and community to facilitate the school's goal setting
- collect and organize baseline data after goals are set, help teams measure the results of proposed changes, and evaluate results once these are implemented
- reorganize data for various district/state reports
- build colleagues' confidence in understanding and using data while also diminishing the threat that data often pose
- know the school and its needs, know the questions teachers want to ask, know the students, and have a vested interest in the continuing success of "our" school
- be prepared to adhere to shorter feedback cycles by providing monthly reports that give ongoing formative assessments of the school's efforts

As with Holly and Lange's (2001) work with data coaches, Killion and Bellamy (2000) contend that, when creating such a role, it is important to attend to such issues as selection, training, financial and administrator support, and connectedness to the decision-making channels of the school. In a similar vein, Noyce, Perda, and Traver (2000) argue that each district should ensure the requisite building-level expertise by training at least one individual in each school. This approach, they say, is powerful because it places information analysis directly in the hands of those responsible for making and effecting decisions. This strategy also frees up time for more complex analysis by anyone employed to analyze data at the district level.

Such data analysts may well find themselves in **data-using teams**. For instance, Noyce, Perda, and Traver (2000) explain the importance of establishing—especially in a larger school system—a central **data team** (similar to and probably overlapping with Killion and Bellamy's school improvement leadership team). This team lies at the heart of district operations: it relies on input from teachers, but is also linked to the district's central office. Such a team, say the same authors, is very much part of the formation of a data-driven culture that is both localized and systemic. The members of such a team

- are linked with all parts of the local system
- are representative of local stakeholder groups
- are trained in the creation, analysis, and use of data
- may perform the training role of data coach with and for colleagues and other staff
- embody, in the words of Noyce, Perda, and Traver (2000), the "institutionalized willingness to use numbers systematically to reveal important patterns and to answer focused questions about policy, methods, and outcomes"
- need to have in their midst data specialists and data analysts

Indeed, according to the same authors, a data-driven culture requires

> ...a few knowledgeable staff members, supportive administrators, and institutionalized procedures for distributing data collection instruments, retrieving data, writing reports, and informing decision-making. Many important queries require only paper, a pencil, and a calculator. More ambitious projects require desktop statistical software and a staff member who knows how to use it. Happily, such software is becoming more affordable, user friendly, and powerful.

Philip Streifer (2001), who has written about and worked extensively in the field of data-based decision making, has suggested that every school district should form what he calls data work teams (similar to Killion and Bellamy's student-focused action teams or school action research teams). Once developed, he says, the district should

- give these teams adequate time to do their work
- encourage the teams to focus on trends in data over time, not one data point
- encourage the teams to use drill-down analyses to identify the root cause of a problem and conduct research on what works to solve the problem
- build a culture that supports the review and use of data for decision making in the school improvement process

Clearly, then, various kinds of data teams can be pivotal in the development of data-based decision making and the generation of data-driven school cultures. Whether performing the role of leadership (coordination and organization) or that of an action-oriented task force (in small or medium-sized districts the same team may well play both roles), data teams are essential for orchestrating and undertaking the kinds of efforts described in this workbook. Indeed, members of data-using teams can use all of the tasks included in this workbook to guide their work. The tasks also have a wider application and can be used by those educators who want to become more data literate and more data-driven in their school improvement efforts.

Noyce, Perda, and Traver (2000) have provided a useful checklist for establishing a data-driven school culture as follows:

Data-Driven School Culture Checklist

What does the district want to know?

Where to look:

- ☐ Current district goals
- ☐ Patterns in data

- ☐ Upcoming district decisions
- ☐ Questions raised by teachers, administrators, or the community

How will the district find out?

What to do:

- ☐ Form data team.
- ☐ Conduct an inventory of data currently available in the district and determine its format (electronic or paper).
- ☐ Assess the technological capacity of the district to manage and analyze data.
- ☐ Determine the extent to which personnel in the district have time, skills, and willingness to engage in data-driven projects.
- ☐ Identify indicators of input, process, and outcome variables related to goals.
- ☐ Determine which additional data are reasonable to collect.
- ☐ Train staff to collect and use data.
- ☐ Analyze and disaggregate data.

What does the district do next?

How to proceed:

- ☐ Establish benchmarks and measure progress toward goals over time.
- ☐ Develop action or school improvement plans.
- ☐ Communicate findings.

(amended from Noyce, Perda, and Traver, 2000)

Preface
Task 1: Assessing Current Performance

Purpose: To use a checklist to take stock of the current status of data-based decision making in the participants' school districts.

Grouping: Work on your own and then meet with your Learning Team.

Directions: Using the amended checklist of Noyce, Perda, and Traver, review and place a checkmark (✓) next to what is already in place in your school district. Place an asterisk (*) next to what needs further development. Use the following space for note taking in preparation for meeting with your Learning Team to share your assessment.

What is in place

What is in need of further development

GROUP PROCESS GUIDE

The PATHWISE: *Data-Driven School Improvement* Series is a set of tools designed to assist teams of teachers and administrators in the process of school improvement. Although an individual wishing to improve teaching and learning in a single classroom could undertake many of the activities, the activities are generally presented in the context of group work. The workbooks are sequential in moving through the school improvement process, and the activities are sequential within each workbook. Each activity is designed to build upon those that precede it and to add to the groundwork for those that follow. This **Group Process Guide** is provided to assist facilitators and team members in making the activities effective in achieving their intended purposes. In some instances the activities are intended to help teams identify areas for school improvement focus; other activities are meant to help the team members hone their skills in the group process.

The completion of activities by a school improvement team (referred to in this text as a Learning Team) should reflect the style and needs of that unique team. For a variety of reasons, different teams will move through the tasks with different time requirements and differing levels of commitment to the specific tasks. Some teams who use the materials may be coming together for the first time; others may be long existing and well functioning prior to using these materials as a guide in the school improvement process. It is important to allow your team to use the activities provided to assist your work, but allow your own style to influence how you accomplish each task.

Stages of Group Development

A brief discussion of the stages of groups may assist teams in identifying their level of development. When a team first begins its work together, it is in the **Forming** stage. At this stage the leader/facilitator must take a strong role as the group is still dependent on the leader for guidance and direction. The team's questions focus on the clarity of the task. The behavior of the team is usually polite, impersonal, and sometimes, guarded. Scott Peck (1987), in his discussion of the stages of community making, has labeled this stage "pseudocommunity." He issues a caution for groups in this stage—there is a tendency to fake it by avoiding any conflict and "being extremely pleasant with one another" (p. 86). School improvement teams should use this polite phase to agree on the task at hand and the ground rules that will guide their work as each task inevitably becomes more challenging.

School teams who are grappling with difficult school improvement issues will, quite naturally, move to the next stage of development—**Storming.** This stage also requires the skill of an effective facilitator along with group process techniques to move effectively through the stage. Peck (1987) aptly calls this stage "chaos" as the inevitable conflicts among members become apparent. Part of the storming aspect of this stage can be attributed to the tendency of team members to attempt to convert others to their way of thinking. A challenge for the facilitator and team members in this stage is to be aware that confrontations in this stage tend to be confronting people, rather than issues. The ground rules agreed upon in the **Forming** stage become useful and necessary at this stage. The chaos that the team feels at this stage is not counterproductive; confronting the differing ideas in the group increases the understanding of each other among the team members. It also allows them to examine the strength that each differing opinion brings to its team's effectiveness.

It is this understanding of their diversity that assists groups in moving to the third stage—**Norming.** As individual team members come to feel understood by the others and come to appreciate the strengths in their colleagues, they are able to "empty" (Peck, 1987) the need to convert others to their way and replace that need with a commitment to finding the collective good for the school. During the **Norming** stage, groups are developing the skill to make group decisions. Procedures for group work become routine and expected. The team is able to give and receive feedback and to confront issues rather than individuals. For many teams, this phase happens so quickly and easily, in comparison to the **Storming** phase, that they find themselves in the fourth stage without recognizing the third.

Stage Four is **Performing**—or "community" in Scott Peck's (1987) terms. At this point the team has matured into a closeness; they are "in community" with one another. Teams that have achieved this level of effectiveness are resourceful, flexible, open, and supportive. They are able to accomplish difficult tasks and make challenging decisions. They share ideas and strategies while respecting the gifts of other team members. The purpose of including this overview of group development in this **Group Process Guide** is twofold. First, it is important that teams understand that *all* groups go through these stages of development to get to the point where they can function most effectively and efficiently. Groups should, therefore, anticipate these stages and not be surprised by the group experiences in each stage. Second, there is a caution about Stage Two—**Storming.** Because *all* groups must go through these stages, the storming cannot be avoided if a team truly desires to become a "performing" team. It is possible to retreat back into the politeness of pseudocommunity, but the team will not function as well or achieve as much if the members are unwilling to do the hard work of becoming a highly functioning team.

Group Process Techniques

Ground Rules

Facilitators and team members can take advantage of a variety of group process techniques to assist them in moving through their development and thereby, ensure that they accomplish their intended purpose—to improve their schools. Most of these strategies and techniques are like the paddles of a war canoe and used only when appropriate and necessary. However, the foundation for all strategies, and therefore necessary at all times, are **GROUND RULES** (sometimes referred to as norms or group behavior expectations). Examples of ground rules are as follows:

- Seek opportunities to be involved.
- Praise others, no putdowns.
- Seek to understand, then to be understood (active listening).
- Include all members (a community feeling).
- Empathize—put yourself in another's place.
- Offer the right to pass.
- Ensure confidentiality—what is said in the group, stays in the group.

Groups should establish the ground rules that enable them to work together respectfully in all phases of development. It is the ground rules that assist a group in working through the storming phase while maintaining the integrity of the group's work.

The Foundational Layer of Teamwork Skills

As stated above, group process strategies will be selected and implemented throughout this workbook depending on the activity to be accomplished. The following list of basic strategies, introduced in the first workbook, *Conceptualizing a New Path*, while an attempt to be comprehensive, is not exclusive. Facilitators and team members are encouraged to use other foundational strategies that they have found to be effective in the school improvement planning process. There are excellent resource materials available that provide further ideas (see, in particular, Johnson and Johnson, 2000, and Garmston and Wellman, 1999). The strategies included below, however, are the ones that will be referenced and utilized in the activities in this workbook.

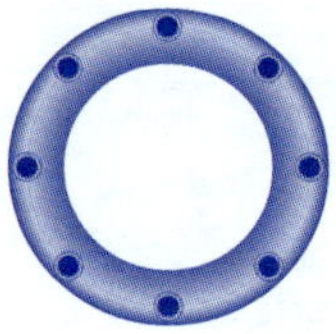

Circle Configuration

The physical arrangement for the team when working should be as close to a circle as possible. Each member of the group should be able to easily hear all others when they speak. The facilitator should sit (not stand) in the circle. All members of the team have an equal voice and equal responsibility for the success of the team.

Groupings

In order to provide team members with the opportunity to reflect and clarify their own thinking as well as to understand that of the other team members, a variety of groupings within the team should be used during activities. At times, individuals should reflect on their own. Dyads (pairs) should be used to allow all members to share their ideas in the safety of a single partnership. Triads (groups of three) can be used for the same purpose. At times it is very effective to reflect alone, then share the reflections in a dyad or triad with that subgroup coming to consensus on their position. Then dyads can be combined into quads with further clarification and consensus on issues. Groups can continue to combine with other groups until one or two larger groups have been able to find their common ground...and thus the common ground for the team.

Facilitation Skills

It is critical that all team members have the opportunity to gain facilitation skills including reflective listening, clarifying, open questioning, summarizing, encouraging, and reporting. Many teams prefer to rotate the role of the facilitator among members; other teams agree on a single facilitator for a specific period of time. Other important team roles include chairperson, process observer, recorder/reporter, critical friend, engaged participant, and, when required, translator. Garmston (2002) emphasizes that having all participants understand and agree to meeting roles is one of his five standards for successful meetings; the other four, all relevant for this **Group Process Guide**, are as follows:

- Address only one topic at a time.
- Use only one process (strategy) at a time.
- Achieve interactive and balanced participation.
- Use cognitive conflict productively.

The above commentary is a summary of the basic skills of facilitation. Later in the **Group Process Guide**, there is a more comprehensive discussion about facilitation skills in the context of team meetings (see School Improvement Meetings).

Go Round

Research has shown that those who speak aloud in the early part of any meeting are more likely to continue to speak and share throughout the meeting. The guidelines for a Go Round are that each person in the group responds to the prompt, in turn, without interruption or comment from the other members. Go Rounds are encouraged at the beginning of each session to bring all members into the group. Go Rounds can also be used at any time to get a sense of what each member of the group is thinking—or when one or two members tend to dominate the discussion, to ensure that *all* ideas have the opportunity to be shared. Go Rounds are an excellent strategy for mobilizing the interactive and balanced participation recommended by Garmston (2002).

Team Listing

For some group activities, it is important to have one team member record each participant's ideas, suggestions, and/or opinions on poster-sized paper. This Team Listing can be posted on the wall for easy reference and revision as needed.

Consensus Building

It is important to define consensus. Teams sometimes create problems (perhaps an intentional block to their success) by defining consensus as *everyone* in complete agreement on a course of action. While an admirable goal, this is rarely achieved. A more manageable definition of consensus is that of "sufficient consensus," defined as agreement among all members of the team that they will not sabotage the implementation of a course of action that is supported by the majority, even though there may be some skepticism regarding the likelihood of its success.

There are a variety of strategies that can be used to facilitate consensus and to determine if a majority opinion exists for a course of action. A Go Round with members stating their position on a scale of 1 (low support) to 10 (high support) can be very effective. Another technique is to have each member (on a count of three) give a signal, such as "thumbs up" for support; "thumb horizontal" for ambivalence; and "thumbs down" for non-support.

There are also many published strategies for creating a consensus opinion. These are available in many books on team building and group work. Examples include cooperative processing, nominal group technique, and brainstorming which will be discussed later in this workbook.

The Tambourine

This is an excellent group processing technique that can be used to enable a group of educators to meld their individual agendas and to find common ground. The technique is called the Tambourine because it resembles a tambourine when drawn on a large sheet of poster paper. The technique works as follows: the members of the group sit in a half circle around the sheet of paper—which can be pinned to a wall or affixed to a stand. It should look like the design below.

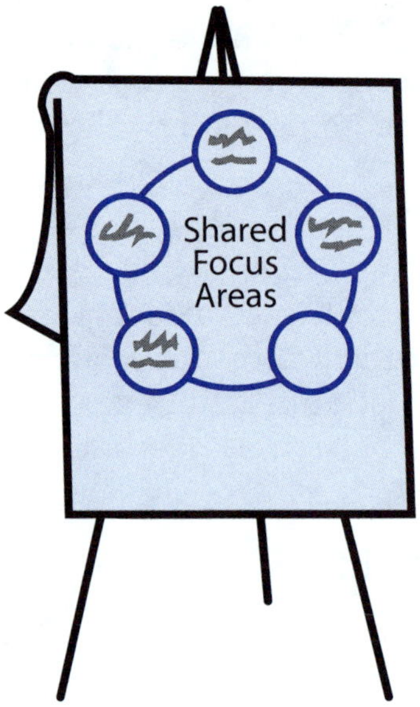

Then each individual, after careful consideration of the issues at hand, goes through his or her list of personal thoughts and ideas. The recorder/scribe writes these on the poster—within the small circle representing this particular member. This step is repeated for each individual until all the small circles are completed. Ten minutes are then devoted to silent scrutiny of what has been produced so far—with an eye to finding the "common ground" issues. Then, using a Go Round, members identify those items that are predominately in common and, if the majority of participants agree, the items are added to the inside of the larger circle—thus producing a shared agenda of common ground issues to which everyone has contributed.

Confronting Issues

Sometimes referred to as dealing with the "elephant in the living room," groups must be willing and able to identify those things that pose barriers to their effectiveness and to openly discuss the issues and seek mutually beneficial solutions. Confronting issues will often throw a team into chaos (the **Storming** phase) and can seem like a setback when a team has appeared to be functioning well. However, if the stages of group processing are thought of as a spiral, each time a group cycles through the phases they emerge at a higher level on the spiral than the last time around. Although difficult and challenging, it is the act of confronting barrier issues that increases the likelihood of long-term success of any team. The ground rules again become critical in helping the group discuss their problems and find solutions.

Celebrations and Closure

On an ongoing basis, groups should engage in celebrations of their accomplishments and as closure at the conclusion of their work. These celebrations should be as public as possible and should recognize the contributions of all team members. The nature of each celebration is determined by the culture of the group—from solemn, ceremonial celebrations to more party-like atmospheres.

The quality of shared decision making based on data is dependent on the quality of collaborative processes used. This **Group Process Guide** is intended to give teams the tools they need to develop quality group-work sessions. Teams are also encouraged to use other sources of group processing strategies and to avail themselves of learning/training opportunities for facilitation skills if available.

Techniques for Generating Ideas and Information Sharing

During the ongoing process of school improvement, there is a recurring need for team members to generate ideas and share information. Several techniques for generating ideas and information sharing are summarized below.

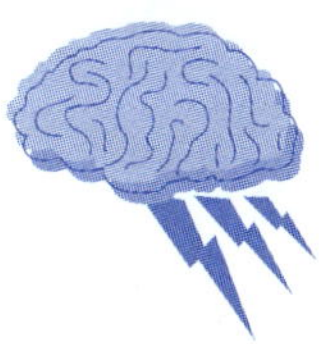

Brainstorming

According to *Pocket Tools for Education* (1996), brainstorming is the free, uninhibited generation of ideas, usually in a group setting, and is used to solicit ideas from the group members on a given topic. In terms of running a brainstorming session, it is important to follow these four steps: select a recorder and group facilitator, generate ideas, record the ideas, and organize the results.

The goals of brainstorming as described in the same publication are to

- generate a wide variety and extensive number of ideas
- ensure that everyone on the team becomes involved in the problem-solving process

- ensure that nothing is overlooked
- create an atmosphere of creativity and openness

In addition, the group facilitator should maintain the following rules:

- No criticism allowed.
- Equal opportunity to express ideas.
- Quantity over quality.
- Piggybacking or hitchhiking (adding to, elaborating or supporting someone else's idea) is encouraged.

Two variations on the brainstorming theme are described below.

Free-Wheel Brainstorm

Individuals are encouraged to spontaneously call out responses, remembering to abide by the following B.R.A.I.N. guidelines:

- Build on each other's ideas.
- Refrain from judgment.
- Aim for quantity.
- Imagine creatively and "out of the box."
- Note all suggestions.

Round-Robin Brainstorm

Each participant takes a turn in giving an idea or suggestion. An individual may "pass" at any time and may re-enter the process to give a response—again, at any time. Continue going from person to person in the group until everyone passes. Once again, the B.R.A.I.N. guidelines should be applied.

Round Robin

The round-robin approach can be used for purposes other than brainstorming and generating ideas (e.g., expressing personal opinions or sharing information). It is important to follow the agreed upon rules and, in so doing, protect each speaker and his/her contribution.

Directions for conducting a Round Robin: Designate a person to start (e.g., the person to the left of the facilitator or the person with a birthday nearest to the current date). Go around in a circle, giving each person a turn to share his/her opinions or information concerning the topic in question. There should be no response from anyone else, with the exception that the group member recording each contribution may ask questions for clarification.

The facilitator should model for all participants a non-judgmental attitude in listening. Attention should be focused on the speaker and what he/she has to say, with the facilitator remembering to avoid making negative or positive responses to the statements. The reason for this strict adherence to limited responses is that other participants might hear the response as limiting their contribution (thinking that what they've got to say will either be treated just as negatively or not viewed in such a positive light).

Round Table

The same procedure as for a Round Robin is followed with the exception that the opinions/ideas are first written on index cards or self-adhering notes and then shared.

Turn to Your Partner

Formulate: Think of your own answer individually.

Share: Share thoughts with one other person.

Listen: Listen carefully to another person's ideas/explanations.

Combine: Build on each other's thoughts and ideas.

Team Discussion

Talk it over; share your ideas. The important focus of the team discussion is that the team has a goal in mind; a specific outcome from the discussion such as, "What do we believe will be the best measure of success of our students' mastery of reading comprehension?"

Three-Step Interview

Group of 4–6 divided into pairs (dyads)

Interview: Set time limit per partner interview and round robin (usually 3–5 minutes per interview and 8–10 minutes for sharing).

Step One: Partner 1 interviews Partner 2
Partner 3 interviews Partner 4

Step Two: Reverse roles

Step Three: Each person shares the partner's response with the whole group (round robin) or with another dyad.

SCHOOL IMPROVEMENT MEETINGS

Structuring Learning Team Meetings

Before the meeting...

Adequate preparation before each team meeting by both the facilitator and team members will result in more productive team meetings. Based on the length of each team meeting, the facilitator must decide what material will be covered in the meeting and what material participants will need to cover on their own in preparation for the meeting. For example, in preparing for the first meeting, the facilitator might ask team members to read on their own, prior to meeting, the Preface and the first section of Chapter One.

The facilitator must also decide which tasks/activities will be implemented in any given meeting. Each task in the workbook is organized as follows:

Purpose: (Why are we doing this task?)

Grouping: (How are we to work—on our own, in pairs or triads, or with the whole Learning Team?)

Group process strategy: (Which strategy will most effectively support us in accomplishing the work we are doing?)

Directions: (What are we doing?)

It is important for the facilitator to carefully study these four elements of a task prior to the meeting to ensure a smooth implementation of the task. Each group process strategy is explained in the **Group Process Guide**, which will serve as a handy reference throughout the use of the workbook. In addition, it is the facilitator's responsibility to ensure that any necessary materials, such as poster paper and markers, are ready for use.

During the meeting...

The group processing skills that have just been covered in the **Group Process Guide** are most frequently used in meetings. Indeed, it is in meetings that school improvement work is generally processed. For the benefit of all those concerned, such meetings need to be focused, purposeful, task-oriented, and productive. There is nothing that gives school improvement a bad name more than meetings that meander aimlessly into educators' personal time. Meetings—and the time used for meetings—are resources that we cannot afford to squander. At any school improvement meeting, therefore, the basic skills and techniques learned and applied in the first workbook, *Conceptualizing a New Path*, need to be practiced in combination to provide for structure, flow, and, above all, task completion. In each meeting, these simple procedural rules should be utilized:

- Assign team member roles.
- Review the ground rules.
- Conduct a focus activity or "ice-breaker."
- Review the goal(s) of the meeting and check for understanding.
- Select an appropriate process to match and accomplish the task.
- Record the conversation by displaying the key words and phrases used.
- Provide time to reflect at the end of the meeting.

Indeed, this checklist is a very handy tool for group facilitators to use when planning school improvement meetings. Moreover, during the reflection time at the end of the meeting, it may well be advisable to invite team members to evaluate the session using the kind of review sheet found on the next page.

Team Self-Review Sheet

For each of the following statements, circle the number which best indicates your view of how your group performed, using the continuum of "1" (Strongly Disagree) to "10" (Strongly Agree).

1. **Objectivity:** We were clear about the purposes and objectives of the task.

1 2 3 4 5 6 7 8 9 10
Strongly Disagree — Strongly Agree

2. **Information:** The necessary information was obtained and effectively used.

1 2 3 4 5 6 7 8 9 10

3. **Organization:** Our team's organization was suitable for the task.

1 2 3 4 5 6 7 8 9 10

4. **Appropriateness:** Our decision-making techniques were appropriate.

1 2 3 4 5 6 7 8 9 10

5. **Participation:** Everyone participated fully.

1 2 3 4 5 6 7 8 9 10

6. **Leadership:** Leadership was exercised appropriately.

1 2 3 4 5 6 7 8 9 10

7. **Openness:** Feelings and opinions were openly expressed.

1 2 3 4 5 6 7 8 9 10

8. **Time Management:** Time was well used.

1 2 3 4 5 6 7 8 9 10

9. **Collaboration:** I enjoyed working in the group.

1 2 3 4 5 6 7 8 9 10
Strongly Disagree — Strongly Agree

10. What might the team do differently to improve the next meeting?

A Closer Examination of Facilitation Skills

Given the task orientation of the teamwork, the countless meetings that underpin the school improvement process, and the concomitant need for productivity, the success of school improvement teams cannot be left to chance. While Weisbord and Janoff (1995) maintain that the members of "self-managed groups"—that come together during one-time brainstorming workshops or planning sessions—can organize their own work without a facilitator at their table, in the kind of ongoing teamwork envisioned in this series of workbooks, the role of the facilitator (whether rotated or not) and the application of facilitation skills are seen as absolutely vital. Indeed, in their pathfinding work on group processing (*The Adaptive School*, 1999) Garmston and Wellman have emphasized the crucial importance of the facilitator's role. In terms that go to the heart of this workbook series, they identify the core values that should guide the process of facilitation:

- **Valid information**

  People share all information relevant to an issue, using specific examples so that others can determine independently if the information is true. People understand the information given to them.

- **Free and informed choice**

  People can define their own objectives and the methods for achieving them and that their choices are based on valid information.

- **Internal commitment to the choice**

  People feel personally responsible for the choices they make.

Moreover, argue Garmston and Wellman (1999), facilitators should be able to call on a knowledge base that includes understanding of Self, Groups, Strategies and Moves, and Maps (see chart on the following page). According to Garmston and Wellman, the facilitator's knowledge of "Self" includes a self-examination using such questions as

- Who am I? What do I care about? How much do I dare?
- Who is my client? For whom am I working?
- What are my desired outcomes in this setting?
- How is my expertise simultaneously an asset and a liability?
- How can I distinguish between being right and being effective?
- What lenses do I wear?
- What types of capacities do I need to develop for this assignment?

This list of questions includes a timely warning to any facilitator—there may be things that he/she says or does that potentially impede rather than enhance the group process.

In terms of knowledge about "Strategies and Moves," Garmston and Wellman (1999) argue that the facilitator should understand how to "Manage Energy," "Manage Information," and "Manage Actions." These distinctions are crucial for an understanding of how teams (and their facilitators) should go about processing school improvement issues. "Managing Energy" involves getting the team members mobilized to work together. "Managing Information" is concerned with the generation and organization of ideas. "Managing Actions" entails deciding what to do with the ideas. In addition, the same authors provide a most useful self-assessment instrument for a facilitator to use when reflecting on his/her role performance, as shown on the following page.

Knowledge Base for Facilitators

MAPS

Facilitators seek to understand meetings and make decisions affecting meeting dynamics with the aid of four types of mental models:

1. Universal meeting goals
2. Structures for meeting success
3. Energy management
4. Principles of effective meeting transactions, information processing, and interventions

SELF

Facilitators' most sensitive and critical asset is themselves. Self-knowledge of cognitive style, educational beliefs, emotional states, intentions, strengths, and limitations permits facilitation decisions to be based on group needs rather than personal preferences.

STRATEGIES AND MOVES

Facilitators manage and direct meeting processes. They know and use a range of facilitation strategies and moves to manage group: energy, information, and action.

GROUPS

Although all groups have common tendencies, each group has unique characteristics that facilitators must take into account: culture, developmental level, group dynamics and history, relationship with facilitator, external environment, and conflicting demands.

Garmston and Wellman (1999)

PAYING ATTENTION TO THE FACILITATION PROCESS

	Notes and Reflections
Clarifies the purpose	
Creates ownership for the proposed challenge	
Checks assumptions	
Clarifies and reinforces norms	
Establishes the process	
Sets time frames	
Stays neutral and objective	
Paraphrases appropriately	
Acts lively and positively	
Makes clear notes	
Asks effective probing questions	
Makes helpful process suggestions	
Encourages participation	
Addresses conflict	
Sets an effective pace	
Checks the process	
Transitions smoothly to new topics	
Makes clear and timely summaries	
Knows when to stop	

Garmston and Wellman (1999)

A Word About Teams

This workbook can be used on two levels: in off-site school improvement training sessions where the participants may or may not be from the same school or school district, or during on-site school improvement planning sessions where the teams will be the site-based teams mentioned in the introduction. Whichever is the case, participants will get the most out of this workbook when they are members of a locally based team and are using the various tasks "for real" (i.e., they are using this workbook to actually do school improvement).

Participants—whether working directly in their schools or returning to their schools following the training sessions—may well want to work within the protection of the kind of Operational Agreement recommended in the first workbook in this series. An example is as follows:

This school encourages students, parents, staff, and community members to put forth a sincere effort to interact in the following ways:

- Have the best interests of our students as a central focus at all times.
- Be flexible and receptive to others' ideas through
  - active listening
  - honest and open exchange of ideas
  - sensitivity in the use of humor
  - acceptance of disagreements as a necessary part of the decision-making process
- Work toward inclusiveness by encouraging and welcoming the involvement of all.
- Respect the integrity of decisions made by other individuals and groups.

Establishing such a school-wide Operational Agreement is a high priority task for any teams embarking on the journey of school improvement.

CHAPTER 1

CHAPTER ONE: INTRODUCTION

School Districts as High Performing Systems

Recent editions of educational journals have described the efforts of school districts across the nation that, even before the onset of *No Child Left Behind*, were recognizing the need to reduce achievement gaps between student sub-populations and to become data driven in the process. For instance, in the October 2002 edition of *Strategies*, a Panasonic Foundation/American Association of School Administrators (AASA) publication, the work of three districts nationwide (Sacramento, CA; South Pasadena, CA; and Charlotte-Mecklenburg, NC) is described. In a previous edition, Broward County, FL, Chula Vista, CA, and San Diego City Schools had been featured. According to the lead article in the October 2002 edition of *Strategies* entitled "All Means All," the districts studied were on their way to becoming high performance systems.

> **Although an increasing number of districts are making significant progress toward becoming high-performance systems, to our knowledge none that are serving a diverse population in the United States have so far achieved that status—that is, if you define a high-performance school system as one where the overwhelming majority of students in all schools are meeting high standards of learning regardless of students' ethnic or socioeconomic background and where the district decisively and effectively intervenes in schools where student performance is persistently low. What seems crucial at this juncture is to learn from the districts that have made substantive progress and to build on the lessons that their stories contain.**

As the article explains, looking at the six case histories, a number of factors are found that are common to all; some other factors are also identified that are common to most of the sites. The five common factors are as follows:

- The school system accepts that its overriding purpose is to enable all students in all schools to achieve high standards and then aligns all policies and activities (including resource allocation and professional development) with this central purpose.
- System leaders hold themselves, their central office colleagues, building principals, and faculty members accountable for achieving the central purpose.

- Professional development for school people is intensive, ongoing, and job-embedded.
- The district ensures that health and social services are made available to students and families in need.
- And, crucially, **data are systematically gathered and analyzed at the system and school levels for the monitoring of progress and identification of needs and challenges**.

Common Attributes

Most of the six districts featured in *Strategies* also have several additional factors in common:

- Multiple forms of assessment are used to measure the academic performance of students.
- An intense focus on core subjects (literacy and mathematics) is reflected in the allocation of instructional time and professional development activities and the adoption of a uniform, district-wide curriculum.
- Preschool opportunities are provided for the most needy students.
- Low-performing schools are given intense support.
- After-school, Saturday, and/or summer instructional opportunities are provided for those students in need of additional support.

It should be noted that the editor of *Strategies*, Scott Thompson, has since coalesced these two sets of points into an eight-item list of the "critical success factors" necessary for a high-performance school system in a recent article in *Phi Delta Kappan* (2003).

Introduction
Task 1: Reviewing Progress

Purpose: To review the progress made by school districts toward being data-driven high performing systems.

Grouping: Work on your own and then meet with your Learning Team. Select a group recorder.

Group process strategy: Use a consensus strategy to come to agreement on strengths and weaknesses (see the **Group Process Guide**). Have the group recorder create the two consensus lists as described under Directions—Part 3.

Directions:

Part 1. On your own and using the following checklist, rate your district's current performance on each factor using a 1 to 5 scale with a rating of 1 = "Strongly Disagree" to a rating of 5 = "Strongly Agree."

Rating

_____ All activities are aligned with the central purpose of achieving high standards for all students.

_____ System leaders hold themselves and their colleagues accountable for achieving this central purpose.

_____ Professional development is intensive, ongoing, and job-embedded.

_____ Health and social services are made available to students and families in need.

_____ Data are systematically gathered and analyzed to identify needs and monitor progress.

_____ Multiple forms of assessment are used to measure the academic performance of students.

_____ An intense focus on core subjects is reflected in resource allocation and curriculum organization and delivery.

_____ Preschool opportunities are provided for most needy students.

_____ Low-performing schools are given intense support.

_____ After-school, Saturday, and summer opportunities offer students additional support.

Part 2. Identify below what you see as your district's key strengths and biggest concerns.

Strengths	Concerns

Part 3. Collate your individual responses into a team score for each item.

Then discuss and come to consensus on which items emerged as **strengths** and which as **concerns.** Have the group recorder record these strengths and concerns on poster-sized paper for the group to review and reflect upon.

To Centralize or Decentralize at the Local Level

Another issue pertaining to the same six districts—whether to decentralize or re-centralize—is not so clear-cut. Two of the six districts (the smallest ones) are the most committed to decentralization in the form of school-based, shared decision making, while two others—Sacramento included—have re-centralized decision-making authority, especially in terms of curriculum and instruction. The *Strategies* article concludes that, while the fact that all four districts have made impressive progress in narrowing the achievement gap might indicate that the degree of centralized decision making is not a critical success factor, the topic warrants further study.

The Sacramento Story

In Sacramento, Superintendent James Sweeney has led the march "from chaos to achievement." Grounded in a clear understanding of how to use core beliefs and data-based accountability as the basis for promoting change, Sweeney, along with board and cabinet members, established an "Action Plan for Educating All Students" in 1998. This plan has several elements, as follow:

1. One element has become known as the "Seven Vital Signs" and consists of indicators (success criteria) against which the district's progress would be judged. Indicators were established in the following seven areas: readiness for kindergarten; student attendance; reading; mathematics; English-language learners; high school graduation rates; and transitions to college and the job market. All schools were held accountable for ensuring that 90% of their students achieved the applicable indicators by 2001. According to Sweeney, "The 'Vital Signs' gave us a common language, a way of talking about achievement that was ours, not the state's."

2. Another element of the plan focuses on the creation of an accountability system for reaching the district's mathematics and reading goals. Five levels of school achievement were established, based on the percentage of students in a building who were reading at or above the 50th percentile on standardized tests. The levels ranged from Exemplary Schools—those with 80% of their students meeting the 50th percentile standard—to Schools in Achievement Crisis with less than 20 percent of their students satisfying the requirements.

3. Having established what had to be attained, nine components were selected as the most likely vehicles for achieving success. These are the so-called "Puzzle Pieces": site-based decision making and budgeting, community support and services, high standards, accountability for results, core beliefs and trust, instruction, data-driven culture, parent participation, and staff development.

It is the district's **data-driven culture**, however, that has enabled those involved to operationalize the demands for accountability and to monitor the implementation of the strategic plan on an ongoing basis. Sweeney and his colleagues are determined that this plan will not end up on a shelf gathering dust, like so many others before it. Consequently, the following actions are in place:

- The school board meets quarterly to review data that track progress toward the district's goals.

- School performance (for reading, mathematics, and attendance) is constantly measured and every school has to account for its annual levels of achievement.

- Schools are given "stretch goals" and annual performance targets (based on the proportion of students who move from one quartile to the next on the standardized tests). Attendance and graduation rates are factored in. Those schools that meet their targets are publicly recognized, while those that do not achieve their targets receive coaching for principals and teachers and assistance in developing improvement plans.

- Every principal is made acutely aware of the levels of achievement and stretch goals for his or her school. The district collects and makes available the achievement quartile breakdowns for every school, as well the scores on reading assessments conducted every six weeks in the elementary schools. The schools' progress in meeting district goals is then addressed in one-on-one sessions that associate superintendents have twice a year with every principal.

- In the elementary schools, a process for examining student assessment data and monitoring student progress has been established through what are called academic conferences. School principals and grade level teams meet four times a year in full-day sessions to review student portfolios and test scores and to develop individual student learning plans.

- The district has also implemented what are referred to as focus school reviews. An associate superintendent and the district's Instructional Learning Support Team make three-day visits to low-performing elementary schools with their reviews including classroom observation and interviews with the principal, teachers, and sometimes parents, and focusing on the three core areas of instruction: reading, mathematics, and English language development. A report on the team's findings is delivered to the whole staff and a follow-up review conducted within a year.

Alignment of programs and resources with the district's goals and intensive efforts to provide accountability for results are two central elements of this local system's improvement efforts. What is being attempted is what most other districts have failed to do: close the stubborn achievement gap between privileged and under-served children.

Equity, Not Equality

As the *Strategies* article points out, this plan is being implemented in the interests of equity, not equality. It quotes Edmund Burke's assertion: "The equal treatment of unequals is the greatest injustice of all." If *equality*, says the article, means that all students and all schools receive the same opportunities, supports, and resources, then the achievement gaps will remain and may well increase. What is required is a serious commitment to equity—*equity* meaning that students and schools are provided with support and resources to meet their unique needs. This distinction between equality and equity, it is pointed out, is especially crucial in the context of standards-based accountability. Standards constitute a common finish line for all students. A race cannot be called fair, however, because it has a common finish line when the runners begin the race from dramatically different starting points. What is required are differentiated activities, supports, and resources for those students and their schools that face a longer, harder, or more uphill race. In Sacramento, for instance, middle school and high school students who are falling behind in terms of their achievement levels in reading and mathematics are identified, in data, and then provided with intensive remedial intervention programs.

Introduction
Task 2: Similarities and Differences

Purpose: To consider the progress made in local districts in light of the Sacramento experience.

Grouping: Work with your Learning Team, first in pairs and then with the whole group.

Group process strategy: Use the Go Round (refer to the **Group Process Guide**) to share.

Directions: Reading this description of the school improvement efforts in Sacramento, how does the work of your district compare? In the space below note the similarities and differences and be prepared to share your lists with your group.

Similarities	Differences

The Pella Story

Another district case study that speaks to the themes of this workbook is that of Pella Schools in Iowa. According to Jane Sanborn (2002), when Superintendent Mark Wittmer arrived in 1999, he set himself a dual task—improving student achievement (which was already on the high side) and garnering teacher ownership in the process. Consequently, four planning teams (containing teachers and administrators) were established to address the key issues of assessment, research, staff development, and technology. While all four teams were charged with collecting, analyzing, and using data for planning purposes, it was the assessment team that was given the primary responsibility of creating a **data system**.

A key outcome of the early team meetings was the establishment of a **profile**. This profile, says Sanborn, does the following things:

- It clarifies the district-wide goals for student achievement and acts as an internal progress report.
- It continues to be the basis of all planning, especially for professional development.
- It includes student grades and test scores by grade levels, attendance rates, and other measures of behavior and performance.
- It is complemented by standards-based report cards that show how well students perform against every benchmark.
- It enables those involved to review data that take them inside classrooms. What was found was that overall class scores were high, but that, as always, good aggregate data can mask pockets of under-performance. Sanborn describes this process of disaggregation as looking at the micro and not just the macro.

By conducting item analysis and looking within the district, school, and classroom test scores for evidence of students' performance in specific skill areas, it was found, for example, that many students were weak in one particular area of early reading skill—phoneme segmentation—which is the ability to isolate sounds from a stream of speech. Test results showed only 30% of the students scored at the proficiency level (the 40th percentile or above).

To address this situation, an action plan was created and, as a consequence, teachers were given professional development support from the local intermediate agency. In what Sanborn refers to as "targeted, tailored training," teachers learned about strategies to use, how to implement them in their classrooms, and how to monitor their impact. Tested one year later, she says, 80% of the students scored at the proficient level or above on this specific item. On the heels of this success, teams now annually review goals, screen their assessment data to identify similar problem areas, update action plans, and organize targeted professional development activities in much the same way as Stephanie Hirsh has recently recommended. Staff development that improves the learning of all students, says Hirsh (2003), uses disaggregated student data to determine adult learning priorities, monitor progress, and help sustain continuous improvement.

Three ingredients are adding to the power of the approaches used in Pella:

1. The introduction of a web-based data retrieval system (customized from an off-the-shelf database program) allows all qualified personnel to easily access district, school, and classroom data. As Sanborn points out, efficiency is one of the many benefits of such a system. While teachers can write inquiries and run reports for their entire class or for individual students, test results delivered in the morning are available to teachers and administrators by the afternoon.

2. As Wittmer intended, staff ownership, commitment, and collaboration have all grown as a result of these activities. What has really helped has been the new in-service format used in Pella. According to Sanborn, one-shot workshops prior to the school year have been replaced by an ongoing mini-course structure (similar to action research) that has three clear advantages: a) teachers are helped to learn a strategy (to be used in the area of identified need); b) they are then encouraged to try it in their classrooms; and c) they are given opportunities to discuss the strategy, its implementation, and its effectiveness with peers at follow-up meetings and to receive collegial, ongoing support and practical advice.

3. Customization of the kind practiced in Pella ultimately leads to personalization. Whereas one-shot workshops assume that every teacher and all their students have the same need(s), as needs identification becomes more sophisticated, as more data are disaggregated, and as remedial interventions are increasingly targeted to the specific identified needs, customization produces personalization. Needs are identified and interventions mounted on a kid-by-kid basis, which is the most advanced form of equity provision.

Reading the case histories of districts like Sacramento and Pella, it becomes clear that the following operating principles are being applied intentionally and consistently:

- Everything is aligned with the guiding vision. Indeed, *alignment* is a crucial concept in these local school systems.

- Accountability for results ensures that the vision is not a set of empty promises. Beginning with the end in mind (Covey, 1989), indicators of success have been established and all subsequent efforts are judged in the light of this conceptual yardstick. Moreover, in order to move toward the success indicators, targets have been established for every sub-system (in Sacramento, these are referred to as "stretch goals").

- The indicators of success include the major assertion that the vast majority of students will meet high standards of learning regardless of their ethnic and socioeconomic backgrounds.
- As a consequence, decisive and intensive interventions are mounted to reduce the achievement gaps between the various sub-populations of students. This work includes an intense focus on core academic subjects, the identification of instructional strategies with proven worth, and sustained professional development in support of these efforts.
- Such a local system is data-driven. In Sacramento, data drive nearly everything that happens. At any point in time, data provide the evidence that can be set against the success indicators to gauge how much progress has been made. Data feed continuous improvement.
- Such districts are rapidly becoming the kind of local data-using systems envisioned in this workbook. These systems establish a set of core processes for continuous improvement:
    - **Clear expectations** are established.
    - Time is found for **regular progress reviews**, the intent of which is **formative evaluation** involving the **diagnostic and reflective screening** of data.
    - New or revised **goals and individual growth plans** emerge.
    - The implementation of the plans is **closely monitored**, including ongoing feedback on performance.
    - This step leads to more **summative evaluations** of the quality and extent of progress over time.

These seven highlighted steps constitute the process dimension of the model explored in this workbook. The steps, when followed progressively and developmentally, have appreciable **effects**:

Establish clear expectations

Find time for regular progress reviews

Focus on formative evaluation as the purpose

Examine and reflect upon the data

Commit to revised goals and growth plans

Take responsibility for implementing and monitoring the plans

Summatively review progress in terms of the achievement of desired learner outcomes

Introduction
Task 3: Reflecting on the EFFECTS Model

Purpose: To reflect on the potential power of the EFFECTS model.

Grouping: Reflect on your own and then meet with your Learning Team.

Directions: Use the following questions for individual reflection and then as a discussion point with your group: When it comes to improving student achievement, why, in specific terms, is this EFFECTS model likely to have the desired outcomes? Is anything missing from the model? Record your reflections in the following space.

Reasons for positive outcomes:

Data-Using Systems—Three Sets of Theory

The substantive model that is explored in this workbook is grounded in three related knowledge bases: systems theory, information management systems, and the continuous improvement approaches associated with Total Quality Management (TQM).

1. Systems Theory

Peter Senge (1990) has argued that systems theory is the "fifth discipline" of learning organizations. He explains:

> As the world becomes more interconnected and business becomes more complex and dynamic, work must become more 'learningful.' It is no longer sufficient to have one person learning for the organization, a Ford or a Sloan or a Watson. It's just not possible any longer to "figure it out" from the top, and have

> everyone else following the orders of the 'grand strategist.' **The organizations that will truly excel in the future will be the organizations that discover how to tap people's commitment and capacity to learn at all levels in an organization.**

In engineering, says Senge, when an idea moves from an invention to an innovation, diverse "component technologies" come together. This process is what is happening to the idea of a learning organization and the chief component technology being applied is systems thinking. Senge (1990) defines the latter as follows:

> Business and other human endeavors are also systems. They, too, are bound by invisible fabrics of interrelated actions, which often take years to fully play out their effects on each other. Since we are part of that lacework ourselves it's doubly hard to see the whole pattern of change. Instead, we tend to focus on snapshots of isolated parts of the system, and wonder why our deepest problems never seem to get solved. Systems thinking is a conceptual framework, a body of knowledge and tools that has been developed over the past fifty years, to make the full patterns clearer, and to help us see how to change them effectively.

Systems Thinking helps us understand two things: first, that all the parts of a system are interconnected; second, as a consequence, change in one part of a system has unintended repercussions in other parts of the same system. Senge uses the analogy of a rug merchant who notices there is a bump in the carpet he is trying to sell. He jumps on the bump, only for it to reappear elsewhere. When this process is repeated several times over, the salesman finally lifts up the corner of the carpet and a large snake slithers out across the floor. What he is describing here is the Law of Compensating Feedback first identified by Jay Forester.

Forester was a computer pioneer who shifted fields to develop what he called "system dynamics." He maintained that the causes of many pressing public issues lay in the very well-intentioned policies designed to alleviate them. Policymakers, he said, are lured into interventions that focus on obvious symptoms, not underlying causes, with the short-term benefits actually fostering the need for still more symptomatic interventions. As with the carpet salesman analogy, solutions merely shift problems from one part of a system to another, probably exacerbating the problem (certainly angering the snake!) in the process.

This, says Senge, is the Law of Compensating Feedback at work: well-intentioned interventions call forth responses from the system that offset the benefits of the intervention. To make matters worse, two contributory factors add to the problem. First, by blaming others for our mistakes, we fail to see that our actions have consequences that come back to hurt us. We misperceive these new problems as externally caused and fail to see how we contribute to our own problems. Indeed, the introduction of *No Child Left Behind* can be viewed in this light—not as something that is externally-mandated but as something caused by our own lack of initiative. Second, blinded by our early (probably superficial) success, when problems emerge we try more of the same.

> **When our initial efforts fail to produce lasting improvements, we "push harder"—faithful, as was Boxer [in George Orwell's *Animal Farm*], to the creed that hard work will overcome all obstacles, all the while blinding ourselves to how we are contributing to the obstacles ourselves (Senge, 1990).**

Introduction
Task 4: The Law of Compensating Feedback

Purpose: To apply the Law of Compensating Feedback to everyday experiences in order to achieve deeper understanding.

Grouping: Work with your Learning Team.

Directions: In your team, reflect on and then share personal work experiences in which your own actions may have triggered the Law of Compensating Feedback, even though this may not have been apparent to you at the time. Then, discuss how being aware of this phenomenon can help us on a daily basis in our professional lives.

The Positive Side of Systems Thinking

Systems Thinking encourages us, through the exercise of data, to see the patterns and interconnections in our systems, to look for root causes rather than surface-level issues (although the one can lead us to the other), and to understand our own role in problem creation.

Moreover, in applying some of these understandings, Systems Thinking can also be used positively and proactively in order to reap the benefits of interconnectedness and synergism—the understanding being that the whole is more than the sum of the parts.

2. Information Management Systems

Alison Cromey (2001) points out that, according to Dooley (1997), three prominent models of organizational change (systems theory, population ecology, and information processing) share a common need for information about the system to guide decision making. In the case of information processing, she says, feedback loops are required to inform decision making. Then, add the power of electronic, computerized information processing to the mix and the results become dramatic—especially in terms of information-creation *in real time*. Indeed, key terms now used on an everyday basis had their origins in electronic approaches to information management. In an article entitled *The Lingo of Data-Driven Decisions* (in the AASA's *School Administrator* Web Edition, December 2002), several terms are explained that are drawn from the publication *Using Data to Improve Schools: What's Working*:

Data mining: the analysis of data for relationships that previously have not been discovered.

Data warehousing: the creation and use of a central repository for all or significant parts of the data that a system collects. A data warehouse typically is a data base or collection of data bases existing in virtual, rather than physical, space.

Decision support system: a computer program application that analyzes and presents data so users can make decisions more easily.

Disaggregated data: data that are broken down by specific student subgroups such as current grade, race, previous achievements, gender, or socioeconomic status.

Formative assessment: assessment in which learning and growth are measured at several points during the learning/developmental process, with the primary intention of obtaining information to guide further teaching/learning steps.

Longitudinal data: data measured consistently from year to year to track progress, growth, and change over time.

Perception data: data that inform educators about parent, student, and staff perceptions about the learning environment and which can reveal areas in need of improvement.

Qualitative data: data based on information gathered using qualitative research methods (interviews, focus groups, observations, and so on).

Quantitative data: data based on "hard numbers" such as enrollment figures, dropout rates, and standardized test scores.

Summative assessment: an assessment at the end of a period of learning/development that sums up how the learner has performed.

Data Drill-Downs

What could be added to such a list are **data drill-downs**. Using data disaggregation, these are intensive attempts to trace the specific root causes of a problem. For example, using this drill-down approach, a superintendent could discover which fourth grade students are not reading at grade level, to which demographic groups they belong, which elements of reading they find the most troublesome, and what correlations may be important (for example, attendance, incidence of disruptive behavior, negative attitudes to school, and so forth).

As a result of such an approach, a specific group—such as fourth grade boys who have reading problems (mainly decoding)—may be identified as becoming increasingly frustrated and disruptive in class, belonging to the same ethnic group, and, yet, being very fluent in their native language. Armed with this information, the district can mount an intensive intervention program aimed at this very specific sub-population of students and the issues facing it. Moreover, over time, the progress of this specific group could be monitored in such data as reading probes and test scores, attendance, discipline referrals, and teacher observations and anecdotal records concerning the identification of changing student attitudes.

Introduction
Task 5: Data Drill-Downs

Purpose: To provide evidence of similar approaches to data drill-downs being conducted in the participants' schools and districts.

LT

Grouping: Work with your Learning Team.

Directions: As a team, recall and describe similar attempts in your school(s)/district(s) to deal with the learning problems of specific groups of students and the role that data played in these efforts. Identify and discuss why these efforts have been successful or not.

3. TQM and Continuous Improvement

Jay Bostingl (1992) has explained the centrality of continuous improvement in the theories of Total Quality Management (TQM). Indeed, he advocates for those in schools to apply four tenets of TQM thinking:

Tenet 1: In Total Quality organizations, including Schools of Quality, all individuals must be dedicated to self-improvement and the betterment of other people in their spheres of influence. This is what the Japanese call *kaizen*, a never-ending journey of improvement for oneself and one's family, friends, work-mates, and fellow community members. Schools of Quality, says Bostingl, view the cyclical learning process as a spiral, with students' and teachers' energies directed toward unlimited continuous improvement. In such schools, learning for everyone—students, teachers, administrators, and other staff—is viewed as a journey, not a series of destinations. Thus, he says:

> The School of Quality is a **true learning organization** in which everyone is dedicated to continuous improvement of self, others, and the processes and systems of everyday life. In the classroom, teachers and students take time at the end of each unit to figure out how they did their work together, and how their collective and individual efforts might be fine-tuned in the following unit to maximize success and optimize collective and individual learning processes and systems....Just as employees of many "learning" companies in Japan and the United States come together in Quality Circles [QCs] on a regular basis to study ways of improving their individual and collective efforts, at some Schools of Quality, teachers, administrators, and other staff members are beginning to meet in QCs to discover ways of improving individually and collectively in their work with each other and with the students and other stakeholders. Teacher QCs most often meet on school time to discuss new ideas garnered from readings about their discipline and education in general.

Tenet 2: What often occurs in such school teams, says Bostingl, is benchmarking—the monitoring of successful educational experiments elsewhere as external standards against which to judge current internal progress and as possible models from which to learn and adopt new ideas. Benchmarking is gaining favor, says Bostingl, because it encourages continuous improvement.

Tenet 3: Quality products in schools, as in businesses, come from quality processes. In Schools of Quality, everyone understands that the improvement of student outcomes can only be improved, over the long run, when learning processes are being continuously improved by those on the front lines and when the entire system supporting those processes is being continuously improved by administrators who create the context for optimal success within the school. According to Bostingl:

> The same systems/process orientation necessary for Schools of Quality to establish networks of support in their quest for *kaizen* at a macro level is essential for learning and improvement to be optimized at the micro level, within each student. Research at the University of California over the past two decades shows that the deepest, most long-lasting learning takes place when it is confluent learning, merging the affective, cognitive, and psychomotor dimensions of learning....We now know that the three elements of the personal internal learning system are interlinked, and they work as processes within the larger human system.

Tenet 4: As part of continuous improvement, there is a major need to be constantly gathering feedback information from all those involved and to use this feedback to constantly modify your systems and processes. This approach, says Bostingl (1992), is helpful to everyone throughout the school system, including students learning how to monitor their own educational processes, bus drivers trying to reduce the time variations of their bus runs, administrators seeking outside funding for school projects, teachers planning new initiatives to support greater student successes, and parents and community members supporting their schools' continuous improvement processes.

When he talks about feedback information guiding continuous improvement, Bostingl is, of course, emphasizing the data-driven nature of the enterprise.

Applying the Three Sets of Theory

Led by these three sets of theory (systems theory; information management systems; and TQM and continuous improvement), therefore, it can be concluded that school systems—as learning organizations—attain integrity in three major ways: by having the same **common properties/processes** being applied at **various system levels** and while constantly nourished by **multiple kinds of data**.

Blackpool Rock meets the Russian dolls...

Two related analogies will help at this point.

1. In England, at every seaside resort, you can find a form of candy known as "rock." It is a rock-hard, mint-tasting, round, cylindrical bar which is pink on the outside and white on the inside and which has the name of the seaside resort

running all the way through it. No matter how much of the bar is bitten off, the name of the town still appears at the end of the bar. Because this type of candy was first produced in the Lancashire resort of Blackpool, it is known generically as "Blackpool Rock."

It is the same for a system. Given that the common properties and processes are at work throughout the various layers of the system, wherever and whenever you examine a slice of the system, you should see the same common properties at work. These common processes provide the internal strength that comes with congruence, consistency, and, ultimately, integrity. As a teacher remarked recently, it is these common properties that constitute the DNA of a local system.

2. Many tourists, when they return from the countries that constitute what was formerly the USSR, bring back the same gift for friends and relatives: Russian dolls. These ornate doll-like effigies are wearing traditional garments and are interlocking: as they get smaller and smaller, each one fits snugly inside the other so that, eventually, all the dolls fit inside the largest which may be six inches or more in height. Each doll is identical, except for its size.

   This analogy speaks to the interlocking, interconnected nature of a system and the need for alignment with the guiding vision through the application at multiple levels of the common properties and processes that are continually fueled by various kinds of data.

The Common Properties

These are the EFFECTS processes of continuous improvement identified earlier in this chapter as follows:

Establish clear expectations

Find time for regular progress reviews

Focus on formative evaluation as the purpose

Examine and reflect upon the data

Commit to revised goals and growth plans

Take responsibility for implementing and monitoring the plans

Summatively review progress in terms of the achievement of desired learner outcomes

Multiple System Levels

Alison Cromey (2001) has pointed out that schools rest within a multi-layered system that consists of the student/teacher dyad, classroom, school, district, community, and state. In previous workbooks in this series, the multiple levels of the local educational system were identified as follows:

- The Student Level
- The Teacher/Classroom Level
- The School Level
- The District Level

Increasingly, these four local levels of educational development are being matched and reinforced by three further levels:

- The Regional Support Level
- The State Level
- The Federal Level

Data-based decision making can occur at any one of these system levels using aggregates or disaggregates of the same data. Moreover, as Denis Doyle (2002) has recently pointed out, the same data (he cites attendance, demographics, test scores, teacher characteristics, school spending, and course-taking patterns) can be used for both diagnostic, i.e., developmental, and accountability purposes. He also identifies a principle of data use that is a vital ingredient of this workbook. In reflecting on the question, "What is the proper locus of data-driven decision making?" Doyle introduces the concept of subsidiarity, which means making the decision as close to the problem as possible. This involves, he says, pushing decision making down the organizational hierarchy as close to the workforce as possible, thus empowering teachers and administrators to be the decision makers.

It is left to Richard Elmore (2000) to take these arguments one stage further. In what can be best described as a challenging article, he has contended that the best way to begin to provide for external accountability is by establishing an internal accountability system. This involves jettisoning the prevalent culture of "loose coupling" (which he refers to as the bane of education) and the establishment of a standards-based system in every locality. According to Elmore (2000):

> **Standards-Based Reform has a deceptively simple logic: schools and school systems should be held accountable for their contributions to student learning. Society should communicate its**

> expectations for what students should know and be able to do in the form of standards, both for what should be taught and for what students should be able to demonstrate about their learning. School administrators and policy makers, at the state, district, and school level, should regularly evaluate whether teachers are teaching what they are expected to teach and whether students can demonstrate what they are expected to learn. The fundamental unit of accountability should be the school, because that is the organizational unit where teaching and learning actually occurs. Evidence from evaluations of teaching and student performance should be used to improve teaching and learning and, ultimately, to allocate rewards and sanctions....The logic of standards-based reform is fundamentally at odds with the logic of loose-coupling, and this difference is not likely to be resolved in the usual way, by simply bending and assimilating the new policy into the existing institutional structure.

One of the solutions to this problem suggested by Elmore is his version of subsidiarity—what he calls **distributed leadership**. The task, he says, is to widely distribute the responsibility for leadership, while, at the same time, uniting these multiple leaders in a common endeavor. Elmore (2000) explains:

> It is the 'glue' of a common task or goal—improvement of instruction—and a common frame of values for how to approach that task—culture—that keeps distributed leadership from becoming another version of loose coupling....Distributed leadership does not mean that no one is responsible for the overall performance of the organization. It means, rather, that the job of administrative leaders is primarily about enhancing the skills and knowledge of people in the organization, creating a common culture of expectations around the use of those skills and knowledge, holding the various pieces of the organization together in a productive relationship with each other, and holding individuals accountable for their contributions to the collective result.

In another of his challenging articles, Elmore (2002) returns to the theme of establishing an internal accountability system that then takes care of external accountability demands.

Most schools that are successful in responding to external accountability systems have solved the assessment problem themselves. Successful schools have internal intelligence about whether the quality of teaching is what it should be and, frankly, are not particularly surprised by the test results they get back because they already know basically how well they're doing. That's a hard message to get across because so many schools and districts have internalized the idea that the accountability system is about the test and so they're in effect teaching the test as opposed to teaching the curriculum.

Most successful schools work on the internal accountability problem by creating greater coherence within the organization. They work on developing their own measures of whether they think they are succeeding with kids, which may have to do with reviewing student work and discussing it among colleagues. It may have to do with curriculum-based tests that pick up whether students are actually learning what teachers are teaching, as opposed to standardized tests that may or may not be connected to the curriculum.

Introduction
Task 6: Reflecting on Elmore's Arguments

Purpose: To have the opportunity to reflect on Elmore's crucial arguments.

Grouping: Work with your Learning Team. Select a recorder.

Group process strategy: Use a brainstorming strategy (see the **Group Process Guide**). Have the team recorder record significant points from the group discussion and brainstorming.

Directions: Richard Elmore continually challenges educators to rethink many of their hallowed assumptions. As a team, discuss the points he makes above and list the major challenges for all those in local education systems. For each challenge identified, brainstorm possible actions to meet the challenge. Use the space provided on the following page for note taking.

The challenges presented by Richard Elmore — Actions

Various Kinds of Data

Victoria Bernhardt (1998) has argued that the kind of successful schools described by Elmore use student assessment data combined with other kinds of data to make themselves intelligent. She has identified four kinds of data:

1. Student achievement data
2. Demographic data disaggregated for various sub-populations of students
3. Perceptions/customer satisfaction data
4. Process/program data

Data Profiles

Taken together, these four kinds of data can be used to comprise a Data Profile such as the one mentioned in the Pella case study. Such a Data Profile can operate at each system level. Therefore, there can be a

- Student Data Profile
- Teacher/Classroom Data Profile
- School Data Profile
- District Data Profile

Each Data Profile can be structured in the same way using the same four kinds of data and can then be used to guide decision making at each system level, as will be elaborated in this workbook. As illustrated in the following table, a common theme and a common set of data points are indicated at each system level. This evidence-centered design serves to produce a unified, coherent data profile for the entire school district.

THE DATA-BASED SCHOOL SYSTEM			
Student	**Classroom**	**School**	**District**
Current goals based on previous year's data and vision	Current goals based on previous year's data and vision	Current goals based on previous year's data and vision	Current goals based on previous year's data and vision
Data Profile	Data Profile	Data Profile	Data Profile
Reviewing progress on current goals	Reviewing progress on current goals	Reviewing progress on current goals	Reviewing progress on current goals
New goals, based on review of profile data and vision	New goals, based on review of profile data and vision	New goals, based on review of profile data and vision	New goals, based on review of profile data and vision
Action Plans	Action Plans	Action Plans	Action Plans

While the concept of a Data Profile overlaps with, but is not identical to, that of a Portfolio, there are many similarities and the differences are largely academic. If not identical twins, they are certainly siblings. Moreover, there is something elegant (in the design sense), symmetrical, and reinforcing about having the same kind of Data Profile operating at different system levels. As Thomas McGreal said in 1996, when referring to portfolio development for teacher evaluation:

> I see it as part of something much bigger: a movement to re-examine what the school stands for and how we express that to

> **the adults who come to work there every day. We can't pride ourselves on individualizing instruction for students and then treat all adults exactly alike. We can't press teachers to develop alternative sources of assessment to get richer pictures of kids' performance and then evaluate teachers the same way we did in 1950....Evaluation of teachers must fit better with what we're asking teachers to do with kids. We ought to be treating the adults in the school at least as well as we treat the kids.**

Data Profiles—whether for the student, the teacher/classroom, the school, or the district—are used as

- evidence of the progress made and set against the general expectations for growth and learning
- the basis for progress reviews that are regularly scheduled
- the material for formative assessment
- the data base that is examined to identify areas of strength and challenges
- the basis of needs, goals, and action plans that are data-based
- the wherewithal for monitoring the efforts to implement the plan over time

The Data Profiles, at all four system levels, drive the common procedures that constitute the process of continuous improvement.

The three dimensions—Common Properties, Multiple System Levels, and Data Profiles—can be integrated using a tool of Systems Thinking such as matrix planning (see the following illustration).

Systems Thinking

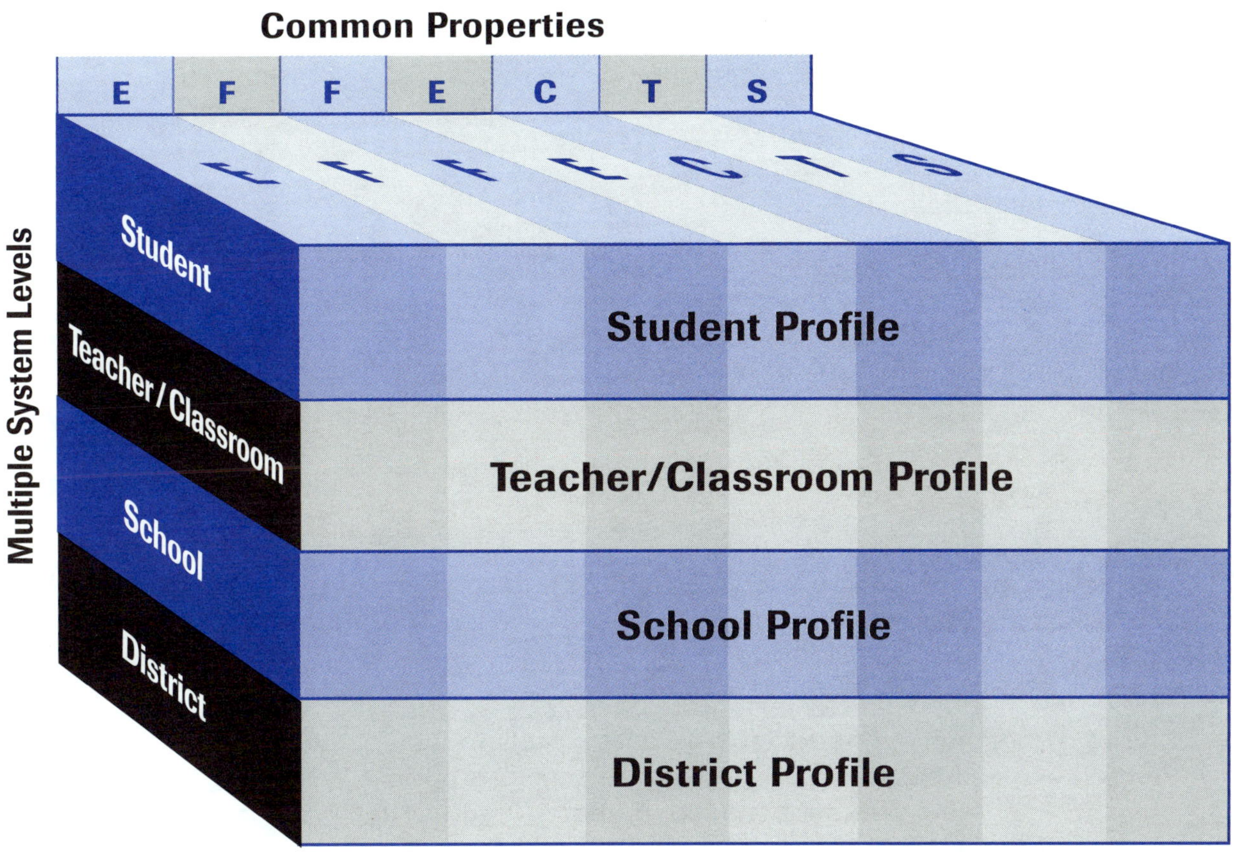

Using Data Profiles at Four System Levels

As the author has argued in this series of workbooks:

- Each Data Profile is a data base, a kind of data-bank account into which deposits, and from which withdrawals, can be made.
- Such transactions are ongoing and continuous; the Data Profile is constantly in use.
- Once created (and continuously updated), the Data Profile can be used to
  - gain new insights
  - make "in-flight" adjustments

- check on progress toward the shared/long-term vision and expectations for learning
- identify changing needs
- rework current goals and/or set new goals
- amend action plans
- monitor progress
- provide, at various times, baseline, up-close, and trend-line data
- show growth over time
- provide the material for accountability
- report to various audiences, both periodically (informally) and annually (formally)

The next four chapters of this workbook are devoted to the use of Data Profiles at each of the four levels of a local school system. At each level, the operating principles remain the same:

1. The ownership, engagement, and active participation of the subject(s) of the Data Profile are strongly encouraged. It is a most appropriate vehicle for putting the "self" into self-assessment. Indeed, Richard Stiggins (1998) has argued that, in the case of students:

   > The teacher is the coach: he or she calls the plays and decides when to have a time-out. The kids play the game; they carry the ball. The responsibility lies with the players. Their **internal control** has to be nurtured.

2. The process of creating and using a Data Profile should be encouraged, supported, resourced, and added to by the level above: consequently, the teacher guides each student; school administrators guide each teacher; district administrators guide those in each school; and state officials and regional support agents guide each district.
3. There is a two-way flow of information between Data Profiles at the various system levels. Disaggregated information for each student can be taken from the teacher/classroom level and presented to each student for use in his/her Data Profile. Working in the other direction, information from individual student level Data Profiles can be aggregated and used at the teacher/classroom level. The

same reciprocal arrangements can be made between the teacher and school levels and the school and district levels. Sometimes the same data (for example, standardized test scores) can be used at all four levels and their meaning interpreted for the individual student, the class, the school, and the district.

4. With the four system levels applying the same operating principles, the benefits of modeling, reinforcement, and team playing come into force—within and across the levels—and the local system is made that much stronger. As Stiggins (1997) points out:

> **Some districts and state licensing boards are even beginning to conceive of portfolios as the basis of teacher and principal evaluation....It may be helpful for your students to see you model the process [of self-reflection] by reviewing, analyzing, and self-evaluating some of your own work.**

Stiggins (1998) returns to this same theme and makes the following observation:

> **If students are working on growth plans, portfolios, and self-assessment, then it makes good sense that teachers should do likewise.**

5. Much of the current practice in this area relates to work on portfolios—for students, teachers, and their schools. As already stated, portfolios and Data Profiles are certainly overlapping concepts and, in practice, may or may not be exactly the same. Data Profiles, in the definition used in this workbook, have to apply to all seven facets of the EFFECTS model of continuous improvement. Portfolios are far more widespread in their use, however, and Data Profiles are only in their infancy and, only then, in some school districts. In order to describe how Data Profiles should be operated, the experience of using portfolios—given their widespread application in schools and classrooms—will be incorporated in each of the following chapters.

Introduction
Task 7: Personal Experiences With Data Profiles

Purpose: To relate what has been said about data profiles to personal experience.

Grouping: Work on your own and then meet with your Learning Team.

Directions:

Part 1: On your own, reflect on your personal experience with profiles/portfolios. Describe those experiences in the space provided below and note the degree of success/satisfaction you have had using them. Did they meet your expectations? What would you do differently in the future in regard to designing and implementing them? What questions do you still have about profiles or portfolios?

Part 2: As a team, share your individual experiences and questions, and then broaden the discussion to include your district's experiences with profiles/portfolios (at various levels of the local educational system). Again, include in your discussion the level of success/satisfaction in using them and whether or not they have met expectations. What would you recommend, as a team, that the district do differently in the future regarding profiles or portfolios?

1. Explain your personal experiences with profiles/portfolios.

2. Would you judge these efforts to have been a success? Why or why not? Be specific.

3. What would you do differently in the future? Why?

4. What questions do you still have about profiles or portfolios?

CHAPTER 2

CHAPTER TWO: USING DATA PROFILES AT THE STUDENT LEVEL

Much of the experience garnered at the student level has been with student portfolios and, in terms of extrapolating the future by building on what already exists, this is definitely the place to start.

In an article entitled "Portfolios Here, Portfolios There—Searching for the Essence of 'Educational Portfolios'," Vicki Kubler LaBoskey (2000) maintains that all age groups of students (her own work that she describes is with kindergarten and college students) can use portfolios productively and their efforts can be used for assessment purposes.

In the kindergarten class attended and described by LaBoskey, portfolios are assembled and discussed on an ongoing basis throughout the school year. They contain student work from two sources: student journals (selected during monthly conferences using a rubric) and work folders (from which selections are made three times in the year). An end-of-year portfolio event involves the students presenting their final portfolios to small groups of parents, friends, and other students. In terms of the college students, much less discussion occurs during the year, but the portfolio presentations have become an important culminating event. Based on her experiences with both age groups, LaBoskey concludes that, for portfolios to be successful, they have to possess four critical features:

1. The process of creating and maintaining a portfolio must be capable of being personalized. It must allow for personal needs to be uncovered, the student's own purposes to be expressed, and individual development to accrue from its use.
2. There must be opportunities to interact about the content and meaning of the portfolios with people who matter and who support the reflective process.
3. Processing portfolios occurs over an extended period of time.
4. The portfolios are constructed and presented within a collaborative context that supports, promotes, and assesses such reflective thinking as a normal part of the students' everyday experience. What is required in schools, concludes LaBoskey, is a "portfolio culture."

Using Student Portfolios in the Classroom

Charlotte Danielson and Leslye Abrutyn (1997) have provided a most useful introduction to using portfolios in the classroom. Portfolios, say the authors, serve multiple purposes. They can be used to engage students in the learning of content, help students learn the skills of reflection and self-evaluation, document student learning (especially in areas that do not lend themselves to traditional assessment), and facilitate communication with parents. Danielson and Abrutyn also point out that most definitions of student portfolios agree that they consist of *collections* of student work that are *purposeful* rather than random and that provide opportunities for students' *reflection* on their work and progress toward agreed upon outcomes.

The same authors point out that there are three kinds of student portfolios: working portfolios (collected works/work in progress); display, showcase, or best works portfolios (examples of "best" work of which the student is most proud); and assessment portfolios (which document what the student has learned). In addition, these three approaches may differ in terms of purpose, audience, and process.

The Benefits of Portfolios

Danielson and Abrutyn (1997) list the benefits of portfolios as accruing in five major areas:

1. Assessment

Portfolios allow for

- more formative, authentic assessment
- outcomes (what students actually know and are able to do) to be assessed
- clarity of expectations
- tracking longitudinal growth—either during one year or from year to year
- students' involvement in the process of assessing their own work and monitoring their progress toward agreed upon goals
- attention to be paid to individuals and their individual needs

  A portfolio is an academic self-portrait that enables the teacher to see beyond the group, thereby enhancing the teacher's awareness of the student as an individual.
- an altered relationship between assessment and instruction

In a portfolio classroom, say the authors, the elements of the instructional process (curriculum, instruction, and assessment) are more intertwined. Curriculum outcomes are established, to be sure. Both instruction and assessment, however, are oriented toward the types of performance through which students can develop and demonstrate their understandings of the skills and knowledge represented by the curriculum. The process is highly iterative, with teacher and students moving forward and backward between instruction and assessment.

2. Instruction

Portfolios, as an instructional tool, allow for

- teaching important skills, including life skills and critical thinking skills
- student awareness of what it takes to accomplish quality work
- increased student engagement and motivation

  As "shareholders" in the learning process, they are encouraged to comment on their own work and that of their peers.
- shared accountability between the teacher and the students themselves
- improved student-teacher communication
- increased use of student metacognition (by reflecting on the learning process) and, therefore, an enhanced sense of identity
- special needs students to demonstrate their growth and accomplishments

3. Parent Communication

Portfolios allow for

- parent comments on the portfolios
- better scrutiny of "evidence" at parent-teacher conferences
- student-led conferences and portfolio evenings

4. Professional Development

Portfolios support professional development as teachers refine their practice, both individually and collectively, by allowing for

- enhanced collegiality—through the process of sharing, assessing, and reflecting on the quality of student work
- quality of expectations/standards for quality work to which both students and teachers are accountable
- serious thought to be put into the quality of the assignments given to students

- feedback on instruction

  Teachers become more aware of the aspects of the curriculum that the students have not mastered. Areas in need of strengthening are identified, which helps teachers in replanning their instruction.

- evaluating student work against quality criteria which the students are made aware of in advance

5. Research

Portfolios allow for

- longitudinal research

  When schools maintain student portfolios over a period of time, teachers can delineate general trends and patterns in terms of student learning.

- cross-sectional research that investigates the work of students at a given point in time

As Danielson and Abrutyn (1997) conclude:

> **Because they provide authentic windows on the learning and thinking of students over time, portfolios allow educators to explore questions of instructional strategies, student reflection, and self-evaluation in ways not possible when more traditional measures of student learning are used. Although educational research has traditionally been the province of the university professor, increasing numbers of practitioners have discovered that they are ideally situated to conduct action research in their own classrooms, both contributing to the profession and receiving recognition for their efforts.**

A major point emerges from this discussion. It is a point that will be repeated at every system level and with every kind of data portfolio/profile. The student at his or her level (like the teacher at his or her level and the school at its level) is not alone. The student, the teacher, and the school are being educated from the level above and, in turn, are helping to educate the level above by demonstrating their support needs.

In terms of a two-way conversation, both levels help each other. Typically, therefore, a student portfolio/profile helps growth and development at two levels. By being a communication tool between student and teacher, the teacher helps the student advance, and the student helps the teacher advance in order to further help the student advance.

It is an iterative learning relationship based on reciprocity. The student's learning is enhanced through feedback from the teacher and his or her own self-reflection and self-monitoring efforts, and the teacher's learning is enhanced through the feedback represented by the student's work. Further support and illumination can also come in the form of critical comments from professional colleagues who have the opportunity to study the same piece of student work.

Moreover, as the Janusian[1] ("boundary") figure in this situation, the teacher is able to look both ways by introducing external, general expectations ("standards") into this learning situation, while knowing in fine detail how each student measures up to these expectations and what has to be done to get each and every student to achieve the desired level of performance. The teacher is the fulcrum between the general and the particular, the practical manifestation of which is diagnostic teaching—the mounting of personalized, needs-based interventions that help each student move toward the general expectations. The portfolio process also helps the teacher identify groups of students with the same needs, thus, leading to needs-based grouping and interventions in the classroom.

In Palo Alto Schools, for example, in California's Silicon Valley (see Lafee, 2002), in what is known as the Kid-by-Kid Program, a student identified as being below grade level is linked to a "quality intervention." This data-driven, data-intensive approach draws upon a host of informational sources (which could be the contents of a data profile): state-mandated test and content standards test results, writing samples, and various diagnostic tests that are given at the beginning of the year to establish baseline activities. One of the program's goals is to monitor the progress of each child throughout the year and the other is diagnostic teaching—targeted, specific, finely-tuned, instructional interventions.

In terms of student portfolios, there is a fine balance to maintain. What is required is a combination of student ownership, motivation, and self-awareness with the teacher acting as the "guide-on-the-side" carefully nurturing and supporting, but taking care not to usurp, the student's centrality in the process.

Data Profiles at the Student Level
Task 1: Reciprocal Benefits of Student Profiles

Purpose: To provide an opportunity for team discussion concerning the reciprocal benefits of student portfolios for both students and teachers in both theory and practice.

LT

Grouping: Work with your Learning Team.

[1] Janus was an ancient Roman god usually represented as having two faces—one looking forward, one looking backward.

Directions: Discuss the following questions with your team:

1. Why is the reciprocal potential of student portfolios so important?
2. In what ways is this potential realized in current practice?
3. What is missing or needs more emphasis?

Robert Marzano on Student Portfolios

Robert Marzano (2000), in his book, *Transforming Classroom Grading*, points out that portfolios are commonly thought of as collections of performance tasks. He quotes Resnick and Resnick (1992) who maintain:

> **In this method, frequently used in the visual and performing arts and other design fields, individuals collect their work over a period of time, select a sample of the collection that they think best represents their capabilities, and submit this portfolio of work to a jury or panel of judges.**

Marzano concludes, however, that portfolios have a wider appeal for three reasons. First, they can be a tool for self-assessment which, he says, is the most underused of assessment methods. Agreeing with Danielson and Abrutyn, he maintains that self-assessment can be a vehicle for the development of higher-order metacognitive skills and the identification of individual learning goals. Second, at the end of a grading period, when students have an opportunity to provide a summative account of how well they did in each topic, each student could provide his/her ratings (using the scoring rubrics supplied by Marzano) and evidence for performance in each area. At this point, says Marzano (2000):

> **Student portfolios might be used quite effectively, because they would contain a "body of evidence" to support students' ratings for each topic. Then, at the end of the grading period, the teachers would have the portfolios and the students' ratings to consider in making their final judgments.**

Third, student portfolios can be used as the vehicle for teachers and students to interact about their respective judgments. In a collaborative dialogue, the teacher and student can jointly analyze the student's strengths and weaknesses **relative to specific outcomes.** Any discrepancies between their ratings can then be discussed in depth.

Data Profiles at the Student Level
Task 2: Using Student Portfolios for Assessment

Purpose: To consider the potential of student portfolios for assessment purposes.

Grouping: Work with your Learning Team. Select a recorder.

Group process strategy: Select a brainstorming strategy. Have the recorder create a team list.

Directions: As a team, brainstorm the ways that student portfolios can be used for assessment purposes while the recorder takes notes. Use the space below for note taking.

Ways that student portfolios can be used for assessment:

Richard Stiggins on Student Portfolios

In his major publication concerning *Student-Centered Classroom Assessment*, Richard Stiggins (1997) definitely supports the idea of student portfolios.

> I regard portfolios as a wonderful idea....However, I do not regard portfolios as a separate assessment method. Rather, they represent an excellent means of collecting diverse evidence of

> **student achievement...and assembling it into a coherent whole. In short, portfolios are a means of communicating about student effort, growth, or achievement status at a point in time.**

In arguing that portfolios are an open, rich, and flexible way to communicate abilities and accomplishments and a more student-involved means of sharing such information, Stiggins recommends the definition of student portfolios provided by Arter and Spandel (1992).

> **A student portfolio is a purposeful collection of student work that tells a story about the student's efforts, progress or achievement in [one or more academic disciplines]. This collection must include student participation in the selection of portfolio content; guidelines for the selection of that material; criteria for judging the merit of the work collected; and evidence of student self-reflection. This definition supports the view that assessment should be continuous, capture a rich array of what students know and can do, involve realistic contexts, communicate to the student and others what is valued, portray the process by which work is accomplished, and be integrated with instruction.**

Stiggins (1997) lists the reasons for the popularity of portfolios:

1. They are diagnostic; they track student achievement over time to reveal improvement and growth or the lack thereof.
2. They preserve the detailed and complex picture of student achievement that is often lost when condensed and translated into a report card grade.
3. They afford students an excellent context within which to take responsibility for maintaining and tracking their own files and records of achievement which, in itself, is a critical life skill.
4. They help students learn to reflect on and see their own improvement as achievers. This involvement has real motivational power.
5. They give students a voice and provide insights into students' academic self-concepts, academic interests, and a sense of their own needs.
6. They provide excellent opportunities for students to practice their reasoning proficiencies, analyze their own work, compare work over time, draw inferences about their growth or needs, and learn evaluative or critical thinking skills.

7. They help students understand the work production requirements of real-life situations, such as developing portfolios for job applications.

8. They can form the basis of the dialogue with parents at student-led conferences and can act as the cornerstone of a student-centered learning environment.

Portfolios, concludes Stiggins, are engaging for students *and* teachers.

Six Keys to Success

Stiggins (1997) argues that there are six key ingredients in constructing quality student portfolios.

1. In order to avoid overload, there should be a clear sense of purpose, a sharp focus and all eyes kept on the agreed upon achievement targets. Stiggins points out, however, that the purpose may change over time and, as a consequence, the material in the portfolio may have to change.

   If a state, district, school, or family wants to maintain a set of portfolios containing the best, most timely evidence of a student's current level of academic achievement, such as for the award of a certificate of mastery or to qualify for graduation, that's fine. This simply means that when a student can provide compelling evidence of a new level of competence with respect to a particular achievement expectation, the old outdated evidence in that portfolio is discarded and the new material replaces it.

   This is particularly likely to be the case when students have to demonstrate the progressive acquisition of standards, benchmarks, and grade level expectations.

2. While aligning the learning targets to the kind of assessment methods that can deliver into the portfolios the information required to show growth and proficiency, those involved should never lose sight of the need for quality assessments. It is vital to apply a consistent commitment to the five standards of assessment quality. According to Stiggins (1997), these are: clear targets, clear purpose, proper methods, sound sampling, and control of bias and distortion.

3. Teachers and their students should be sure of the story the portfolio is to tell and let this understanding guide the selection of material. It is important, says Stiggins, to develop clear guidelines for material selection.

4. There should be explicit criteria for assessing student work. These criteria are the standards against which students and teachers will gauge success. Indeed, Stiggins (1997), in maintaining that teachers must decide in advance and share with their students how the merits of the work in the portfolios will be judged,

comments, "I continue to press the point that students can hit any target that they can see and that holds still for them."

5. The students should be involved in the process of selecting pieces of work for *their* portfolios. Students have a stake in their own future and their portfolio collections will end up in their hands.

6. Periodic student self-reflection on their own achievements should always be encouraged. According to Stiggins (1997), "The simple fact is that students who learn to evaluate their own achievement become better achievers through that process."

   It is through self-reflection, he says, that students maintain contact with their own strengths and weaknesses (relative to external indicators of success), know what it takes to succeed, acquire a vocabulary to use in communicating about success, and keep in touch with accumulating evidence of their own proficiency.

Data Profiles at the Student Level
Task 3: Six Key Ingredients for Student Portfolios

Purpose: To use the six key ingredients for constructing student portfolios for review purposes.

Grouping: Work on your own.

Directions: Using the six key ingredients for constructing student portfolios suggested by Richard Stiggins, evaluate the strength of your current classroom activities (or school/district activities if you are not in the classroom) using a five-point scale, with 1 being "Strongly Disagree" to 5 being "Strongly Agree." For each, include summary comments in the space provided that support/explain your rating.

Rating
My/our student portfolios:

______ 1. Have a clear sense of purpose.

______ 2. Comply with the standards of quality assessment.

______ 3. Are grounded in clear guidelines for material selection.

______ 4. Are accompanied by explicit criteria for assessing student work.

______ 5. Create opportunities for student involvement, e.g., student self-selection of material.

______ 6. Encourage self-reflection on the part of the students.

Echoing Danielson and Abrutyn (1997), both Marzano and Stiggins emphasize the importance of portfolios in encouraging and improving student reflection and self-assessment. Arter and Spandel (1992) have provided these criteria for effective self-reflection:

- **Coverage:** According to a checklist, does the reflection address all relevant criteria?
- **Accuracy:** Are the students developing an accurate sense of their achievement or growth? How do the teacher and student evaluations compare? What are the similarities and differences?
- **Specificity:** Are examples given to support the points made?
- **Revelation:** Does self-reflection bring students to new insights about their learning?
- **Integration:** Do the students generate a synthesis of their insights in order to make broader conclusions about their achievement?

To initiate self-reflection, Stiggins (1997) provides a list of trigger questions (adapted from Arter and Spandel, 1992):

- Describe the steps you went through in completing this assignment. Did this process work and lead to successful completion or were there problems? What would you change next time?
- Did you receive feedback along the way that permitted you to refine your work? Describe your response to the feedback offered: Did you agree or disagree with it? Why? What did you do as a result of this feedback?
- What makes your most effective piece of work different from your least effective? What does your best work tell you about where you have improved and where you need further work?
- What are the strengths of your work in this project?
- What aspects still need more work? What kind of help will you need?

Spandel and Culham (1995) have pointed out that there are various kinds of student portfolios—the differences being largely related to their multiple purposes—which can be used as students move across grades and have to deal with changing expectations.

- **Celebration Portfolio:** This is a keepsake portfolio containing a personal collection of favorite pieces of work and special academic mementos that can be used to communicate the things that the students are most proud of with families. While no external standards are used in this approach (making it appropriate for students in the early grades), by identifying the attributes of the pieces of work and saying what makes them special, the students are working toward standards.

- **Time Sequence Portfolio:** This approach aims to reveal changes or accomplishments in a student's academic performance over time. Two examples are Growth Portfolios and Project Portfolios:

  - **Growth Portfolios:** By including multiple indications of the same proficiency (with the evaluation criteria being held constant over time), these show how proficiency has changed over time.

  - **Project Portfolios:** These depict the completion of the steps in a project conducted over time, including evidence of not just completing all the necessary steps but doing so in a quality manner.

- **Status Report Portfolio:** This approach demonstrates that the student has met certain pre-established standards of performance. A "Passport Portfolio," for instance, makes a case for the student having attained certain levels of proficiency and having reached the necessary achievement targets in order to be able to pass to the next level of his/her education. Such portfolios can be used for admission to college, for the award of a certificate of mastery in high school, and for course completion.

Stiggins (1997) concludes that the greatest strengths of portfolios are three-fold:

1. They can show growth over time, which can be very motivational for the learner. In one particular sixth grade classroom, says Stiggins:

   > [The students] maintain files of all work completed, one for each discipline. When it comes time to assemble work for their growth portfolios in preparation for the periodic student-led parent conferences, the students and teacher meet as a team to select exemplary work. And remember, this is a growth collection, not a status report; the early material may not be very good, but is presented as a baseline from which to show improvement. This teacher wants her students to see their improvement, and she

> wants their parents to see it, too. Portfolios can demonstrate this very effectively.

2. Portfolios can be very comprehensive and provide the opportunity for holistic, richly detailed descriptions of student learning. As Stiggins (1997) explains:

> Portfolios offer a detailed way of communicating about student achievement. In this case the communication arises out of collecting and displaying actual examples of student work. Unlike grades, portfolios maintain the detail needed to tell a complete story of a student's achievement. This does not mean that they should replace grades, but rather that we should see them as serving different but nonetheless important purposes.

3. Student involvement and the development of a learning partnership with the teacher are other real benefits that accrue from the use of portfolios. Stiggins continues:

> Portfolios have gained immense popularity in recent years because of their potential as a teaching tool that offers many opportunities for student involvement. Portfolios diagnose student needs and reveal improvement over time. They can encourage students to take responsibility for their own learning, track that learning, and gain an enhanced sense of academic progress and self-worth. Portfolios help students learn to reflect on their own work, identify strengths and weaknesses, and plan a course of action—critically important life skills. And finally, they give students opportunities for practicing important and useful reasoning and problem-solving skills.

The Limitations of Student Portfolios

1. According to Winograd and Webb (1994), while portfolios are very useful in the classroom and for providing opportunities for student self-assessment, they are not the best tools for large-scale assessments. Other commentators have noted that portfolios are not suitable for the kind of high-stakes testing that is being increasingly demanded of schools and classrooms (Stiggins, 2001).
2. Students' self-selection of material for their portfolios might be good for their ownership and commitment but is problematical when it comes to issues of validity and reliability.

3. As Stiggins (1997) has pointed out, the complexity of the portfolio development process (which involves students in the exercise of several major skill sets) is often underestimated.

4. Too many portfolios, says Stiggins, become bloated "mega-portfolios." Such scrapbooks are stuffed full of material and cease to have any sense of quality or meaning.

5. Portfolio development is time-consuming for both the students and their teachers.

Data Profiles at the Student Level
Task 4: Cost-Benefit Analysis

Purpose: To conduct a cost-benefit analysis of using student portfolios in the classroom.

LT

Grouping: Work with your Learning Team. You might want to consider dividing the group into two sub-teams.

Directions: This is a major task and is a three-step process. Consider having one sub-team work on step one, while the other sub-team works on step two. The whole Learning Team will work on step three.

Step One: In your team (or sub-team), list the **benefits** (the advantages) of using student portfolios as well as the specific situations.

Benefits	Situations

Step Two: In your team (or sub-team), list the **costs** (the disadvantages) of using student portfolios as well as the specific situations.

Costs	Situations

Step Three: Now, with your Learning Team, review the work completed in steps one and two. Weigh the advantages and disadvantages and decide whether, on balance, the advantages outweigh the disadvantages or vice versa and why. Note the reasons for your decision below.

New Moves

Every innovation has pluses and minuses, as in the case of student portfolios. The task then becomes one of finding ways to mitigate the negative factors. Stiggins (1997), for instance, welcomes the introduction of electronic portfolios for students as an "encouraging new development on the horizon." Davies, Cameron, Politano, and Gregory (1992) have recommended the use of cover sheets for each portfolio entry. Such "captions" can be used to explain what has been selected and why—and which external standards are relevant and to which selections. The more accountable students have to be for their selections, the more these selections are tied to external learning expectations, and the more these issues are discussed between students and their teachers, the more valid and reliable the process will become.

Moreover, moves are also under way to bring together large-scale and classroom assessments into a meaningful dialogue. According to the NAESP publication *Essentials for Principals: Data-Based Decision-Making* (2001):

> The standards and accountability movement of the last decade has resulted in the collection of more assessment data about students than ever before. Often, the results from high-stakes tests have been used merely to grade and rank schools and students. Used solely this way, assessment data is of doubtful value in improving student achievement. Educators know this, and many of them have therefore viewed the imposition of state-mandated tests as an unwanted burden that actually stands in the way of school improvement.
>
> But a new trend is now starting to emerge. Education leaders are beginning to see the power of using this same assessment data, along with data gathered from carefully designed classroom-based assessments, to improve instruction at the school, classroom, and student levels.

On the one hand, then, while norm-referenced standardized tests have been mainly used for high-stakes testing and accountability purposes (see McTighe and Ferrara, 1998), they are increasingly being used for this purpose and for improving student learning in the classroom. Moreover, when it comes to improving classroom learning, they are being increasingly used in conjunction with criterion-based, standards-based assessments. On the other hand, as Richard Elmore (2002) and Douglas Reeves (2001) have both argued, by increasing the use of standards-based assessment in the classroom, not only will the students' thinking, reasoning, and communication skills improve, but so will their performance on high-stakes tests.

Marzano (2000) has suggested the use of scoring rubrics in order to integrate various assessments for grading purposes. The same principle could be applied to portfolios, thus allowing them to be "scored" and graded. Indeed, following Marzano's lead, standards and benchmarks can be used as the criteria for both selecting material for student portfolios and the creation of scoring rubrics. Reeves (2001) has suggested:

> When student mastery of academic standards becomes the focus of classroom assessment, there are four significant features. First, student performance is compared to a standard rather than to a norm, an average, or to other students' performances. Second,

> students are required to demonstrate their proficiency. This is an improvement over traditional assessment because guessing a response has little or no value for the teacher or student. Third, standards-based assessments are not veiled in secrecy; what is expected of students is clear to teachers, parents, and students. The gamesmanship typically surrounding test preparation is replaced with a focused curriculum that relates to academic standards. Fourth, the focus of standards-based assessments is the improvement of student learning, not merely the rendering of an evaluation and the announcement of a score.

If, however, as Reeves (2001) maintains, the "key to effective assessment is balance," portfolios can be used to provide evidence of student achievement across a range of assessments, standardized tests included. As we begin to explore how the concept of a Data Profile can be used to enhance current practice with portfolios, one idea is to have a section for each student—guided by the teacher—entitled "My Test Scores and Their Implications for My Learning."

How to Construct a Data Profile at the Student Level

In the interests of systemic congruence and consistency, it is recommended that Victoria Bernhardt's four kinds of data be used as the organizer for a Data Profile at each of the four levels in the local educational system. Starting with the Student Level, then, the first task is to show the relevancy of Bernhardt's model, which was originally designed to operate at the School Level. It is interesting to note Bernhardt's own comments in her preface to *The School Portfolio: A Comprehensive Framework for School Improvement* (1994):

> The schools are so proud of their school portfolios and the progress they have made with this approach that they decided a parallel process had to be developed for teacher improvement. This led each school to design its own rubrics that go deep into the student achievement continuum to describe a continuum of implementation for that school's specific vision. Teachers have taken the process two steps further by developing their own professional portfolios and conducting action research in their classrooms. With this key combination, teachers can describe the impact of specific changes in their classrooms and student achievement increases. These teachers now truly understand the impact of their actions on students and student learning, and how their efforts impact the total learning organization. They also understand that improvement is forever and continuous, and that one cannot collect too much data when trying to understand phenomena.

What is now being suggested in this workbook is another parallel development. Just as the teachers working with Victoria Bernhardt in the project schools recognized the importance of developing professional, teacher-based portfolios, it is important to understand that the next step is to take the idea to the student level and, in so doing, connect with the work on student portfolios summarized earlier in this chapter.

Four Kinds of Data

According to Bernhardt (1998), there are four different kinds of data (what she refers to as "multiple measures"):

Student Learning Data

These are data that focus on student learning results ("multiple measures of student learning"):

- Standardized test scores
- Grade point averages
- Standards-based/criterion-based assessments
- Authentic assessments
- Performance-based assessments/"products" of student learning

Demographic Data

These data provide descriptive information (largely documentary evidence) about the school community, including such elements as

- Enrollment
- Attendance
- Dropout rate
- Discipline referrals
- Grade level
- Ethnicity
- Gender
- Native language

It is these factors that allow for the **disaggregation** of data for various sub-populations of students.

Perceptions Data

These data refer to the perceptions, attitudes, and beliefs of various stakeholder groups—teachers, administrators, students, parents, community members, and so forth. What is elicited here is their thoughts, viewpoints, and, above all, feelings—their reactions to what is going on in the school. Their perceptions are gained by using the following data collection methods:

- Interviews
- Focus groups
- Surveys
- "Fly-on-the-wall" observations

School Processes Data

These data refer to everything that the teachers are doing to get the results they get. School programs, instructional strategies, and classroom practices are all included in this category. Questions such as, "How is reading being taught in the second grade?" and "How thoroughly are the 'Six Traits of Writing' being applied in the middle school?" can be answered by studying these data.

Concerning these four kinds of data, Bernhardt (1998) makes three essential points:

1. All four kinds of data need to be collected and studied **over time** to ascertain whether change and growth are occurring. This is the advantage of gathering **trend-line** data on a **longitudinal** basis.

2. Taken together and thus garnering the benefits of **triangulation**, these measures, says Bernhardt, provide a powerful picture of student learning "in the round" that can help us understand the school's impact on student achievement.

3. In her model, the four categories of data are shown as overlapping circles (see the following illustration). This diagram shows the importance of not only using the different kinds of data in conjunction (triangulation), but also of studying the intersections to gain enhanced, more sophisticated understanding of the pertinent issues.

Data Collection, Analysis, and Goal Setting

MULTIPLE MEASURES OF DATA

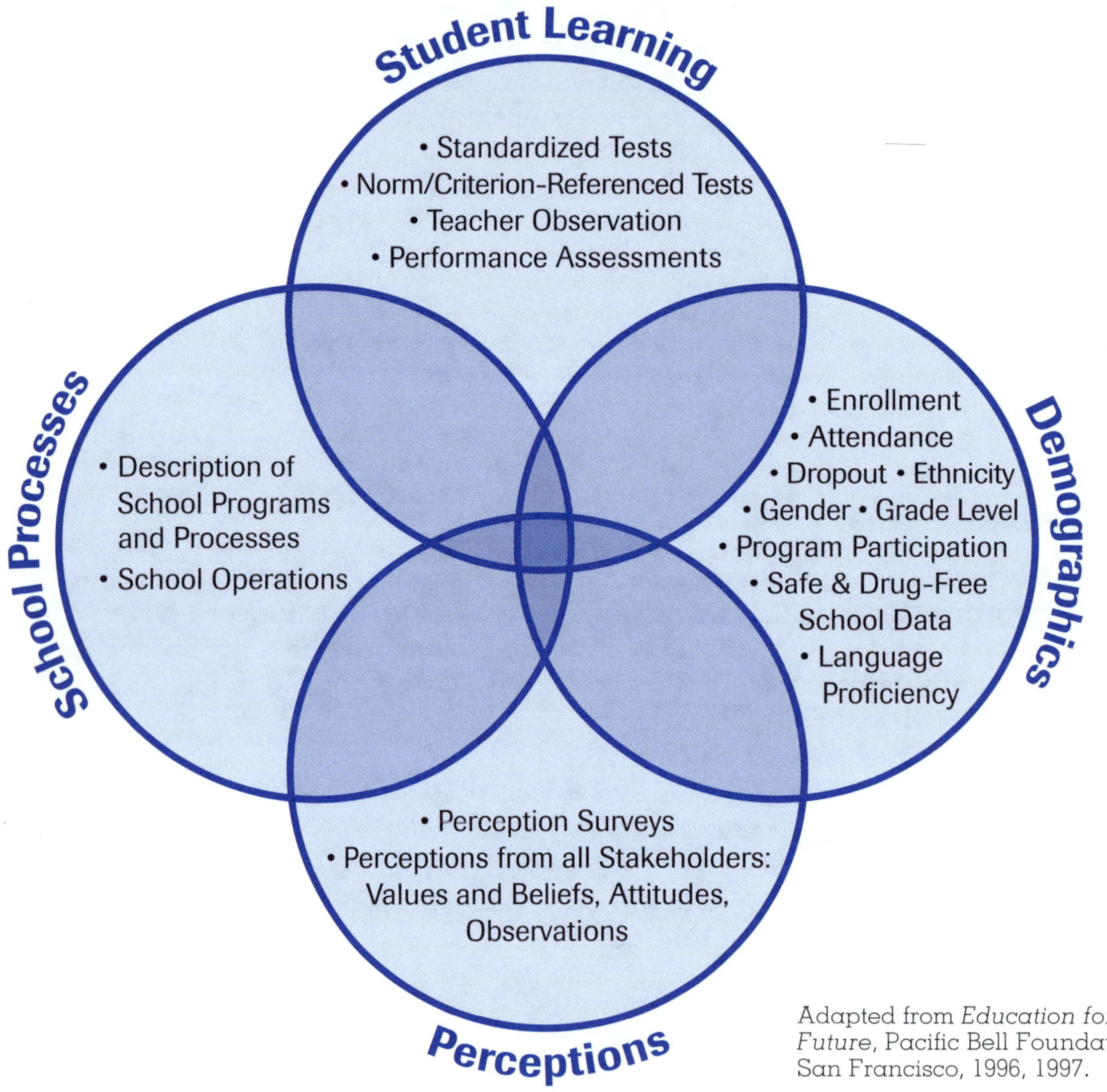

Adapted from *Education for the Future*, Pacific Bell Foundation; San Francisco, 1996, 1997.

Indeed, says Bernhardt, in studying the intersections, it becomes possible to ask the following kinds of questions:

Intersecting Two Categories

- Do students who attend school every day get better grades? (Demographics/Student Learning)

- Is there a gender difference in students' perceptions of the learning environment? (Demographics/Perceptions)
- Is there a difference in how students enrolled in different programs score on a state-mandated test?
(Processes/Student Learning)

Intersecting Three Categories

- Do students of different ethnicities perceive the learning environment differently and score differently on student achievement tests?
(Demographics/Perceptions/Student Learning)
- What program is making the biggest difference with respect to student achievement of at-risk students?
(Processes/Student Learning/Demographics)

Intersecting Four Categories

- Are there differences in achievement scores for boys and girls who report that they like school, by the type of program and grade level in which they are enrolled?
(Student Learning/Perceptions/Processes/Demographics)

Applying Bernhardt's Model to the Student Level

While Bernhardt's model was designed for data gathering and portfolio construction at the school level, it can easily be adapted as a framework for establishing a Data Profile at the student level. This can be done as follows:

Student Learning: How are you doing?

In order to answer this question, each student is asked to respond to these subsidiary questions:

- What are the grade level expectations that relate to your current progress?
- Relative to these expectations, how are you doing?
- How are you doing compared with other students at your grade level?
- Are you happy with your progress?
- What evidence are you using to make these judgments?

- Which are your best pieces of work?
- Why did you make those particular selections?
- What are your strengths and where are you not so strong?
- What do you need to concentrate on to get stronger?
- What are your personal learning goals?
- In addition to your academic goals, in what ways are you trying to improve your personal, interpersonal, and life skills?

Demographics: Who are you?

- How would you describe yourself and your family background?
- Which grade are you in?
- If you are assigned to multiple classes during the day, such as a middle or high school schedule, list these classes.
- Have you received any discipline referrals? If so, how often?
- Do you have good school attendance? If not, why not?
- Have you received any honors in school?
- What are your interests and hobbies?
- In which school clubs and activities are you involved?
- What are your career aspirations?
- Have you worked on a résumé?

Perceptions: What do other people think of you as a learner?

- What kind of feedback have you received from your teacher(s)?
- How do your parents/guardians think you are progressing?
- How do you feel about yourself as a learner?
- Is your school a supportive learning environment?
- In what ways do you contribute to the learning environment of your classroom and school?

Processes: What is working for or against you?

- In terms of all the things that the school is doing to support your learning, what is working for you and what is not working for you?
- How do you learn best? For instance, do you prefer to learn in a group or by yourself? Do you prefer to read about a new idea or learn about it in a more active way?
- Do your teachers take this into account? In what ways?
- Which are your favorite subjects/classes? Why?
- What kind of teaching helps you learn best (such as class discussions, teacher demonstrations, and so on)?
- Would you like more help with your learning? In what ways?
- In terms of your learning, are you sufficiently challenged?
- In terms of your personal learning goals, what can the school do to help you achieve them?

Profile or Portfolio

In this context, it is interesting to note Edie Holcomb's (1999) comments in her book *Getting Excited About Data. How to Combine People, Passion, and Proof* (1999):

> The term *school portfolio* is used here to describe a collection of data compiled at the individual school level....Although it is frequently referred to as a *profile*, I prefer to call it a school portfolio for three reasons. First, I believe that the comparison to a portfolio of student work is very fitting because of the school context. Second, the term *portfolio* is apt because a student's (or artist's) portfolio is intended to demonstrate three important aspects of his or her work: the range of skills, the very best products, and artifacts that provide evidence of progress and learning. A school also needs to present the wide variety of needs it addresses, examples of success to celebrate, and evidence of improvement occurring where needed.
>
> Third, I believe one of the reasons school-level data should be compiled is to paint a more complete picture of the uniqueness of that school and its students than the term implies. Painting a picture requires more than an outline or silhouette. This is not to

> say that a school portfolio should be a two-ton tome. [It is important to] emphasize the need to be selective about its contents, so staff and constituents are not overwhelmed and intimidated by sheer volume.
>
> The relationship between the mission and the school portfolio is that one should provide evidence of the other. In organizational development terminology, it's looking for alignment between our "espoused theories" (beliefs) and our "theories in use" (how we operate on a daily basis). When we provide evidence of what we do, how closely does it match what we say?

Several points emerge from this passage that are central to the purpose of this workbook.

- The concepts of profile and portfolio are very similar, if not interchangeable.
- Edie Holcomb would seem to be a subscriber to the same belief that underscores this entire workbook—that it is reinforcing, synergistic, and elegant (from a design point of view) to have four identical and overlapping collections of data that provide evidence of progress and the basis for future action at the four levels of the local educational system that comprise a school district.
- All the constituents of the local school system—students, teachers (both individually and collectively as a school staff), administrators (at school and district levels), and other stakeholders—should be challenged to compare their progress (as evidenced in the data collections) against their hopes and aspirations. "Where do I/we want to be?" and "How far have I/we progressed toward that desired state as evidenced by the data in my/our profile/portfolio?" are the fundamental questions to keep asking ourselves.
- Learning and change at every level of the local system (Charles Handy maintains they are the same process) are generated by this act of gap analysis: comparing our current progress as evidenced in our data against success criteria that we have created or have been presented to us. These success criteria might take the form of
    - Curriculum standards and benchmarks
    - Grade level expectations
    - Teaching standards, e.g., Danielson's framework for teaching
    - School improvement goals and indicators of success
    - School mission and vision statements

As Leon Festinger (1954) claimed, the object is to establish—through the study of data—"cognitive dissonance" between our expectations (whether self- or externally imposed) and our current level of performance. Knowledge of such performance gaps, it is argued, motivates us to do better, thus leading to gap, dissonance, and discomfort reduction.

- Any kind of gap analysis, however, is only made possible by the generation of shared, general expectations ("standards") for teaching and learning against which any progress has to be set. Student progress is increasingly being described in these terms, which has spawned a mini-revolution in the writing of student report cards (the data for which can be drawn from student data profiles).

Data Profiles at the Student Level
Task 5: Promoting EFFECTS at the Student Level

Purpose: To provide review questions to be asked of the student level.

Grouping: Work on your own and then meet with your Learning Team.

Directions: On your own, review this chapter and reflect on the following question: In what ways can student portfolios/student data profiles promote each aspect of the EFFECTS model? Using the following chart, be as specific as possible as you link student portfolios/student data profiles with the EFFECTS model. Meet with your Learning Team to share completed charts.

EFFECTS	Specific ways that student portfolios/data profiles promote EFFECTS
Establishing clear expectations.	
Feedback being provided to the learners in progress reviews.	
Formatively screening for the purpose of diagnostic intervention.	
Examining, reflecting, and making decisions on the strength of the data.	
Committing to personal goals and growth plans.	
Taking responsibility for implementing and monitoring the plans.	
Summatively assessing progress toward desired learner outcomes.	

CHAPTER 3

CHAPTER THREE: USING DATA PROFILES AT THE TEACHER/CLASSROOM LEVEL

The classroom teacher is the fulcrum of the model explored in this workbook. He or she has three fundamental responsibilities:

1. To encourage, support, guide, and monitor the process of establishing and using Data Profiles/Portfolios at the Student Level.
2. To undertake the compilation of a personal Data Profile/Portfolio that includes the interrelated twin tasks of identifying the strengths and needs of each and every student in the class (and their collective strengths and needs) and intervening accordingly (this can be summed up in the phrase "diagnostic teaching") and identifying his or her instructional strengths and needs against an external set of teaching standards. As mentioned in the previous workbooks, this dualism involves teachers in the Janusian role of looking both inwards (to identify the students' individual and collective needs) and outwards (to identify ways in which they need to enhance their professional practice).
3. To contribute to and use the school portfolio/profile as a faculty member.

Professional Standards

According to Danielson and McGreal (2000), in their seminal text *Teacher Evaluation to Enhance Professional Practice*, there have to be professional standards and evaluative criteria (the "what") against which to judge a teacher's current performance.

> Standards of teaching state what teachers should know and be able to do in the exercise of their profession. People express this concept in one of two fundamental ways: in terms of what teachers do, or in terms of the results they achieve. The former could be called "inputs"—an enumeration of teacher tasks reflecting all the complexity of the work. (These lists of tasks need not be checklists of specific types of behavior, but they identify all the different aspects of teaching that yield high levels of student learning.) The latter, on the other hand, can be considered "outputs"—the results teachers achieve in their work, for example in the extent of student learning or performance, as an indication of the quality of teaching.

> Of these two approaches, the former has the longer history of use in the evaluation of teaching. More recently, however, in response to greater calls for accountability of teachers and whole schools, many districts (some as required by their state legislatures or boards of education) are incorporating measures of student learning into the definition of teaching to be used in evaluation (Danielson and McGreal, 2000).

In the "input" tradition, say the same authors:

> Some states have incorporated criteria for teaching in their licensing procedures. Georgia led the way (in 1980) with the Teacher Performance Assessment Instrument (TPAI), followed by North Carolina, Florida, Connecticut, and other states. Effective teaching, as described by Madeline Hunter (1982) and other researchers, is an example of this tradition that won widespread national attention during the 1980s.
>
> The Educational Testing Service (ETS) drew on these efforts in the development of Praxis III: Classroom Performance Assessments for Licensing Beginning Teachers. The development process incorporated extensive literature reviews, expert panels, job analyses, and pilot and field-testing. More recently, ASCD's book *Enhancing Professional Practice: A Framework for Teaching* (Danielson, 1996) was based on the Praxis III research and linked to the principles of exemplary practice described by the Interstate New Teacher Assessment and Support Consortium (INTASC). The book expands the teaching skills identified in Praxis III to include the work of experienced teachers, and the book reflects the vision of teaching and learning embedded in the work of the National Board for Professional Teaching Standards (NBPTS). This framework, building on the earlier work of others, is the latest effort along these lines; and many school districts have used it as an organizing structure in defining effective teaching and establishing criteria for their evaluation systems.

As Danielson and McGreal explain, the "outputs" approach is far more problematical. While recent research findings have demonstrated that the quality of teaching greatly influences student learning results, how to provide evidence of this fact is far from straightforward. In a standards-based local system, national norm-referenced tests tend to have high reliability (the interpretation is always the same) but rather low validity (whether the test is aligned with what is being taught is somewhat debatable). On the other hand, criterion-based state tests have lower reliability and medium to high validity and classroom-based assessments have very low reliability (due to a lack of inter-rater reliability) and presumably very high validity (they are presumably faithful to what is being taught).

In addition, given that student learning is influenced by many factors beyond the control of schools and most teachers are working with a diversity of learning needs in the classroom, the standardization of such "output" approaches becomes very difficult. According to Danielson and McGreal, it is important to be able to take the baseline levels of student achievement into account—however differential they might be—and to be able to show how much growth each student experiences as a result of the teacher's efforts. One example of how this could be done is to compare writing samples from September to May; they can be collected, say Danielson and McGreal, from the **student portfolios.** This is a major point for this workbook. Teachers can collect material from student portfolios and use them in four ways:

1. Teachers can read and "assess" the extracts and provide evaluative feedback to the students. This might even become an ongoing dialogue.
2. Teachers can use the extracts as evidence of student progress (as described earlier) and place significant examples in their own portfolios.
3. It is in their personal portfolios that teachers can provide evidence of their success with both specific students and the class generally in terms of the grade level expectations for the particular grade in question.
4. This same information can also be used as evidence of the teacher's progress with his or her individual professional growth goals and his or her contributions to the school improvement goals.

At its most basic, say Danielson and McGreal (2000), a **teaching portfolio** is a collection of information about a teacher's practice. It can be used for the twin purposes of teacher evaluation and professional development. The same authors list the key features of a teaching portfolio as identified by Wolf, Lichtenstein, and Stevenson (1997):

- A portfolio should be structured around sound professional teaching standards, and individual and school goals (another example of the merging of general and specific expectations).
- A portfolio should contain carefully selected examples of both student and teacher work that illustrate key features of a teacher's practice.
- The contents of a portfolio should be framed by captions and written commentaries that explain and reflect on the contents of the portfolio.

- A portfolio should be a mentored or coached experience in which the portfolio is used as a basis for ongoing professional conversations with colleagues and supervisors.

Such teacher portfolios can be used both formatively and summatively, but if used for the latter, an assessment component is required containing clear criteria, an established set of valid and reliable scoring rubrics, and extensive training for evaluators in order to assure fairness and reliability. Given these strictures, teacher portfolios are much more likely to be used formatively for the purpose of professional development. Indeed, according to Danielson and McGreal (2000):

> The use of portfolios as a professional development experience, especially for teachers new to a district, would seem to have extraordinary potential. Burke (1997) and Dietz (1998) both contend that portfolios have the capacity to present an authentic view of teaching and learning over time, thus offering a more complete and valid portrait of how teachers think and act. The creation of a teaching portfolio provides teachers, especially beginners, with a structure and a process for documenting and reflecting on their practice. This is the essence of professional learning.

For his part, Burke (1997) argues that professional development portfolios enable educators to do the following:

- Articulate their visions of teaching and learning.
- Develop their professional goals and action plans.
- Select learner-centered goals.
- Interact with peers throughout the process.
- Reflect on what has been achieved and what has been learned along the way.
- Share new insights with others.

Data Profiles at the Teacher/Classroom Level Task 1: Reasons for Teacher Portfolios

Purpose: To provide participants with an opportunity to reflect on the reasons for establishing teacher portfolios.

Grouping: Work with your Learning Team. Select a recorder.

Group process strategy: Use a brainstorming strategy; have your recorder create a team list.

Directions: Having read the commentary above on teaching portfolios, brainstorm a list of reasons why it is important for teachers to create their own portfolios. Also consider possible uses, benefits, and drawbacks to teaching portfolios.

Developing an Effective Teaching Portfolio

In an article entitled *Developing an Effective Teaching Portfolio*, Kenneth Wolf (1996) explains that educators have long used student portfolios to assess student performance but now they are turning their attention to portfolios for teachers. When they are carefully conceived, he says, teaching portfolios can be used to significantly advance a teacher's professional growth (when teachers carefully examine their own practices, those same practices are likely to improve), ensure that evidence of exemplary teaching doesn't vanish without a trace, and provide opportunities for these exemplary practices to be shared with other professionals who can then adopt and adapt the practices for their classrooms. Seen in this light, teaching portfolios might well be the vehicle that has been missing—the platform for networking (Fullan, 1996) and "getting to scale" (Elmore, 1996) the professional dialogue regarding the application of best practices.

Wolf (1996) provides several answers to the question of why the interest in teaching portfolios as follows:

- Although such portfolios can be time-consuming to construct and cumbersome to review, they have the potential of capturing the complexities of professional practice in ways that no other approach can.
- Therefore, says Wolf, they are an effective way to assess teaching quality—certainly, as Danielson and McGreal (2000) maintain, on the "inputs" side of the equation.
- They also provide teachers with opportunities for self-reflection and collegial interaction based on documented episodes of their own teaching. Teacher learning is galvanized by the teacher studying what the students learned and what he or she did or did not do to effectively support the process.

- Teaching portfolios can be used for a variety of purposes at different career stages. They can be used
    - at the college level to demonstrate achievement on teacher education programs;
    - at job interviews;
    - to become eligible for bonuses and advanced certification (for example, the National Board for Professional Teaching Standards [NBPTS] requires the completion and submission of a teaching portfolio);
    - to renew professional licenses;
    - by teachers as architects of their own professional development by having them create portfolios based on individual growth plans.

Wolf (1996) defines a teaching portfolio in much the same terms as Danielson and McGreal. It is, he says, a collection of information about a teacher's practice. A teaching portfolio, however, should be more than a miscellaneous collection of artifacts or an extended list of professional activities. It is important to carefully select the contents of a finished portfolio so that it is manageable, both for the constructor and reviewers. If not carefully thought out, says Wolf, a portfolio can easily take the form of a scrapbook (an ill-assorted collection of mementos) or a steamer trunk (a container of various papers and projects). It should carefully and thoughtfully document a set of accomplishments over an extended period of time and the process of construction should be conducted in the company of mentors and colleagues.

In terms of the contents of a teaching portfolio, Wolf (1996) has some very practical advice. There should be the following components:

- An introductory section that describes the teacher's philosophy and goals
- A middle section containing teaching artifacts and written reflections
  This section should contain a variety of information:
    - Lesson plans
    - Anecdotal records
    - Examples of student projects, assignments, and other work samples
    - Survey responses and their explanation
    - Class newsletters
    - Teachers' written descriptions and videotapes of the instructional process
    - A brief statement (or caption) which identifies the artifact and describes the context in which it was created

- A concluding section containing evidence of ongoing professional development, formal evaluations by supervisors, and letters of recommendation

In terms of portfolio development, Wolf (1996) gives this specific advice:

- Provide an explanation of your educational philosophy and teaching goals.
- Choose specific features of your instructional program to document, annotate each entry/artifact, and include a journal for ongoing written reflections.
- Collaborate with a mentor and/or other colleagues.
- Assemble the portfolio in a form that others can readily examine (for example, a loose-leaf notebook or an electronic version).
- (Self-) Assess the quality of the portfolio.

Data Profiles at the Teacher/Classroom Level
Task 2: Reflecting on Wolf's Commentary

Purpose: To use Kenneth Wolf's comments to deepen understanding of the importance of Teacher Portfolios.

Grouping: Work on your own.

Directions: Having now read Kenneth Wolf's comments and suggestions, what additional reasons for having teacher portfolios have become apparent?

Additional Reasons

Wolf (1996) provides some useful information about developing and organizing a teaching portfolio. He suggests collecting and including three categories of information, as follows:

How to Organize a Teaching Portfolio

Table of Contents

1. Background Information
   - Résumé
   - Background Information on Teacher and Teaching Context
   - Educational Philosophy and Teaching Goals
2. Teaching Artifacts and Reflections
   - Documentation of an Extended Teaching Activity
   - Overview of Unit Goals and Instructional Plan
   - List of Resources Used in Unit
   - Two Consecutive Lesson Plans
   - Videotape of Teaching
   - Student Work Samples
   - Evaluation of Student Work
   - Reflective Commentary by the Teacher
   - Additional Units/Lessons/Student Work as Appropriate
3. Professional Information
   - List of Professional Activities
   - Letters of Recommendation
   - Formal Evaluations

Source: Kenneth Wolf (1996)

Wolf's example of a classroom newsletter, as an artifact in a teacher's portfolio, reveals the type of narrative one might develop to accompany such an artifact, as follows:

Sample Portfolio Caption

Title: Weekly Classroom Newsletter
Date: January 13th, 2003
Name: John Stanford

Description of Context

Students write, edit, and publish this weekly newsletter in the writers' workshop.

Interpretation

This newsletter is one way that I keep parents informed about classroom events. It is also an example of how I engage students in meaningful learning activities.

Additional Comments

Parents told me how they use the newsletter to talk with their children about what is happening in school. I also learn more about what my students find important or newsworthy in class each week.

Source: Kenneth Wolf (1996)

Data Profiles at the Teacher/Classroom Level
Task 3: Applying Wolf's Suggestions to Practice

Purpose: To have the opportunity to apply Wolf's practical suggestions to everyday practice.

Grouping: Work with your Learning Team.

Directions: Looking at Wolf's practical suggestions included above, discuss in your team the feasibility of putting these ideas into action. What would be easy? Difficult? Share your reasons with your Learning Team.

Georgea Sparks Langer (1999) has another take on teacher portfolios. In her mind the portfolio process is tantamount to an action research project. Teachers can use the process of creating teacher portfolios, she says, as a self-assessment tool to improve their instruction. They can create what she calls professional development portfolios that are focused on a classroom-based problem, which leads them through "a systematic reflection process, where they frame the problem, set some goals, and pursue them." This process, she says, is very similar to the action research process and follows "five simple, common sense stages":

1. **Define the Problem**
   Teachers need to identify an issue that has been "bugging them." It is critical that time is taken to properly frame the issue because it steers the whole process.

2. **Specify a Target Goal**
   The task here is twofold: to determine a reasonable goal and to translate the goal into indicators of success by designing a rubric to define how the situation should improve.

3. **Make a Plan to Reach that Goal**
   The next step is the identification of professional development needs and the sequence of steps to take to improve the situation.

4. **Implement the Plan and Collect Data**
   A major task during the implementation stage is to collect evidence and document the changes at both the student and teacher levels. Some artifacts that would demonstrate such progress include:

   - Journal entries
   - Samples of student work
   - Notes about what was learned at teacher workshops

5. **Reflect Upon the Results**
   The final step is to pull all the pieces together, describe what has changed and the results achieved, and reflect on what has been learned from the process. It is the reflective component, says Langer, which is a distinguishing factor and takes the process beyond the construction of a "presentation portfolio."

A Framework for Teaching and Professional Portfolios

In Charlotte Danielson's (1996) definitive text, *Enhancing Professional Practice: A Framework for Teaching*, she explores the potential of professional portfolios. The benefits, she says, are fourfold:

- They generate the same kind of ownership and commitment as students experience when they create their own portfolios.
- In having to select pieces of "best work," those involved are applying, and bringing to the surface, quality criteria.

- These quality criteria constitute the educator's philosophy of what constitutes quality work.
- A professional portfolio provides the opportunity to compare one's practice against an external framework of what constitutes effective teaching. Such a framework, as supplied by Charlotte Danielson, also offers a structure for the compilation of a portfolio. Indeed, a teacher can use a portfolio to document the attainment of the various components of the framework (see Appendix A).

According to Danielson (1996), other purposes of teacher portfolios include:

- self-reflection, analysis, and the application of judgment
- support for mentoring and coaching relationships: using portfolios, she says, extends the conversation beyond visiting each others' rooms and provides a context within which to view the observed lesson
- providing evidence of exemplary practice to strengthen a résumé
- self-selection on the part of the teacher (What a novice teacher selects will be different from that of an experienced colleague.)
- connectedness to school goals (If a school goal relates to writing, then samples showing the growth of student performance over time should be included.)

Data Profiles at the Teacher/Classroom Level
Task 4: Linking Standards With Portfolios

Purpose: To consider the relationship between Danielson's framework for teaching (see Appendix A) and a professional portfolio.

Grouping: Work in pairs, and then meet as a whole group.

Directions: Working in pairs, review the 22 components of professional practice that comprise Danielson's framework for teaching, as well as the elements under each component (see Appendix A). Using the following chart, place a checkmark beside each component for which artifacts could be collected as evidence of one's practice for inclusion in a professional portfolio. Also consider specific examples of evidence/artifacts a teacher might include. It will be helpful to continue to reference Appendix A to review the elements under each component as you brainstorm types of evidence. Record this information in the right-hand column of the chart.

When you have completed this task, note which components were *not* checked and discuss with your partner how a teacher could represent his or her efforts in this area. Meet with your Learning Team to share your work.

✔	Component of Professional Practice	Types of Evidence/Artifacts
	Domain 1: Planning and Preparation	
	1a. Demonstrating Knowledge of Content and Pedagogy	
	1b. Demonstrating Knowledge of Students	
	1c. Selecting Instructional Goals	
	1d. Demonstrating Knowledge of Resources	
	1e. Designing Coherent Instruction	
	1f. Assessing Student Learning	
	Domain 2: The Classroom Environment	
	2a. Creating an Environment of Respect and Rapport	
	2b. Establishing a Culture for Learning	
	2c. Managing Classroom Procedures	
	2d. Managing Student Behavior	
	2e. Organizing Physical Space	
	Domain 3: Instruction	
	3a. Communicating Clearly and Accurately	
	3b. Using Questioning and Discussion Techniques	
	3c. Engaging Students in Learning	
	3d. Providing Feedback to Students	
	3e. Demonstrating Flexibility and Responsiveness	
	Domain 4: Professional Responsibilities	
	4a. Reflecting on Teaching	
	4b. Maintaining Accurate Records	
	4c. Communicating with Families	
	4d. Contributing to the School and District	
	4e. Growing and Developing Professionally	
	4f. Showing Professionalism	

Contents of a Professional Portfolio

Danielson (1996) suggests structuring the contents of a professional portfolio using the four domains of her framework:

Domain 1: Planning and Preparation

- 3-Week Unit Plan: provides evidence of the ability to design coherent instruction.
- Instruction Plan for a Single Lesson: demonstrates the planning of content and procedures, including information about the students, instructional goals, activities the students will do, instructional materials, and projected assessments.
- Samples of Assessment Procedures: provides evidence of the teacher's approach to assessment and alignment with instructional goals.
- Knowledge of Students and Resources Sheet: demonstrates the teacher's skill in learning about students' backgrounds, interests, and cultural heritage as well as the teacher's ability to provide resources appropriate for students' needs.

Domain 2: The Classroom Environment

- Videotape of a Class: provides evidence of the classroom interaction, albeit an imperfect substitute for live observation.
- Documentation: provides evidence of management skills through artifacts such as classroom rules and behavior management plans.

Domain 3: Instruction

- Videotape of a Class: demonstrates the teacher's skill in implementing a lesson plan.
- Observational Notes/Peer Observer Feedback: provides a more in-depth dimension that videotape may be unable to capture.
- Instructional Artifacts of In-Class Assignments and Homework: demonstrate a teacher's skill in engaging students in learning and includes samples of the teacher's directions to the students, materials used, student work, and teacher commentary.
- Samples of Student Work: demonstrates the level of student engagement in an activity or assignment and, when possible, includes teacher feedback.

Domain 4: Professional Responsibilities

- Teacher Reflection Sheet: provides evidence of self-evaluation and reflection concerning whether the instructional goals were met and how to go about teaching the same material again.
- Logs: focus on family contacts, participation in school/district projects, professional contributions, and involvement in professional development activities.
- Research Log: provides a way for teachers to reflect on and explore the effectiveness of various instructional approaches.

For use in schools in Iowa, the author (2002) took the same approach as Danielson and, for each of the four domains of effective teaching, he identified the relevant Iowa Teaching Standards (which were passed into law in 2001) and ways to collect data to provide evidence of effectiveness in each area—data that could be included in a teacher portfolio. Appendix B illustrates this application of the framework and lists the types of evidence that could be collected.

Individual Learning Plans

Although the concept of a Data Profile—whether at the student, teacher, school, or district level—largely involves store-housing information for use in decision making, it is inextricably linked with the idea of improvement planning. Data-driven planning lies at the heart of multi-leveled improvement efforts in schools. Just as a Student Profile can inform goal setting and planning at the individual student level (the equivalent of an IEP for each and every student), so too can each teacher use his or her personal Data Profile to identify needs, improvement goals, and a professional growth plan. The Data Profile may be a component of teacher evaluation and/or professional development activities. Put simply, data come alive when they inform growth and action.

Richardson (2002) has argued that, in the move away from one-size-fits-all staff development to custom-designed, individually-tailored professional development opportunities that are adapted to fit the personal learning style of the recipient, individual learning plans for teachers are becoming increasingly important.

> Just as schools and districts design staff development programs that will help achieve student learning goals, so, too, individual teachers and administrators will want to align their professional growth with desired improvement in student achievement. That means teachers must increasingly become more knowledgeable about the needs of their students and greater advocates for their own learning needs.
>
> More and more districts are requiring teachers to develop individual learning plans. Such individual plans are crucial cogs

> in a system of staff development that links individual learning with school goals and schoolwide learning with district goals. Award-winning districts have long required teachers to develop ILPs. Ohio is requiring teachers to develop IPDPs (Individual Professional Development Plans) as part of new licensure requirements that are being phased in. The IPDPs are based on the needs of the educator and his or her students and must be aligned with school and district goals. Educators who form the Local Professional Development Committee review the plans to ensure that individuals are connecting with those broader goals (Richardson, 2002).

Two points are vital here:

- Individual Learning Plans for teachers are not a license to "do your own thing"; they are informed by looking inward to ascertain the students' specific learning needs relative to what are identified by looking outward—curriculum standards, grade level expectations, school and district goals, and so on. Individual Learning Plans are the epitome of the Janusian role of teachers. They are the meeting point for internal needs and external expectations and where the twin pressures are resolved in the form of one goal statement for a particular teacher in a particular classroom. As Richardson explains, the important concepts here are connectedness and alignment: the plans are connected with and aligned to both the specific students' needs and what's going on more generally in the building and in the district.
- Continuously improving organizations, says Richardson, are staffed with people who are continuously improving. In this workbook this notion is being extended, however, to include continuously improving students who are taught by continuously improving teachers who work in and contribute to continuously improving schools and continuously improving school districts. And the process of continuous improvement hinges on the use of Data Profiles to generate Individual Growth Plans at all four system levels.

According to Richardson (2002), continuous improvement at the teacher level can be generated by following a five-stage process as follows:

Stage One: Examine Data

> Begin your individual learning plan just as schools and districts begin their planning: look at data....Schools and districts take broad looks at data and then they pull apart the numbers and examine them more closely. Individual teachers can do the same thing (Richardson, 2002).

In closely examining data, Richardson suggests that each teacher should take these steps:

- Collect data about the students (including such assessments as weekly quizzes, unit tests, or statewide tests).
- Collate student learning data from several years of classes.
- Disaggregate that data to look at sub-groups of students by gender, ethnicity, race, language backgrounds, poverty, and any other groupings appropriate for the school and community.

  Dennis Fox (2001) provides an excellent example of this kind of specific approach at work in the classroom (see the following pages).
- As the data is examined, look for patterns or trends.
  - Do the students often have difficulty in the same areas?
  - In which areas do they have repeated difficulties?
  - In which of these areas is improvement required?
- Study student products that students create as a result of their assignments (which may well be in their portfolios) and ask the following questions:
  - How closely did the students' products match the learner expectations?
  - Did the students produce the quality of work expected?
  - Were there consistent problems with the products generated?

Stage Two: Summarize What Has Been Learned

The task here is to organize and begin to make sense of the data.

- Richardson suggests writing up to a dozen summary statements about what has been discovered (using one of the four tools included in the Richardson article and included as Appendix C).
- At this stage, she says, only describe identified problems and do not attempt to solve them.

  For example, one of these statements might be: Fourth grade students with non-English-speaking parents are under-achieving in informational writing.
- Then cite the evidence that supports the statement.
- Select the three or four summary statements that link to improvement goals for the school/district.

A Classroom Example

Fox (2001) provides a good example of summarizing and analyzing classroom data in order to improve practice as follows:

A first grade teacher administers a test on rapid word recognition during the first week of December. The students are required to read words in English from a list as accurately and rapidly as possible. The teacher administers the test individually to each of his seventeen students.

The goal for December is thirty-five words, while the goal for the end of the school year is for the students to recognize all of the one hundred words on the list.

Having given the test, the task now is to analyze the outcome data. Some of the findings are as follows:

- Three students exceeded or met the goal of thirty-five words;
- Fourteen students did not meet the goal;
- One student was close (thirty-three words) to the goal;
- None of the seven English language learners met the goal;
- Out of a total of 100 words, the range of scores for recognized words was from 2 to 86 words;
- The student below the one who recognized 33 words recognized 18 words;
- The lowest score was achieved by a native English speaker;
- Three of the English language learners scored in the top half of the class (with a score of 11 or higher);
- One of the students who met the goal scored the minimum of thirty-five;
- Other than the three students who met or exceeded the goal, the disaggregated data indicated there were no significant differences between the performance of native English speakers and English language learners.

Now the teacher's task, says Fox (2001), is twofold: to identify those instructional practices that promote word recognition and to eliminate or revise those practices that are ineffective. This requires that the teacher self-evaluate his teaching, assume some responsibility for his students' performances, and make changes in instruction that are aligned with the various (and different) needs of the students.

Data Profiles at the Teacher/Classroom Level
Task 5: Classroom Data Analysis

Purpose: To respond to Fox's example of classroom data analysis.

Grouping: Work with your Learning Team, first in pairs and then as a whole group.

Group process strategy: Use the Go Round strategy to share examples.

Directions:

Step One: Looking at Dennis Fox's example of a classroom test being analyzed, work in pairs to think of other everyday examples of this kind of specific approach being used. Share and discuss examples with the whole group.

Step Two: With your Learning Team, note the benefits and drawbacks that accrue from such a specific approach to data-based decision making at the classroom level.

Examples

Benefits of Data-Based Decision Making at the Classroom Level

Drawbacks of Data-Based Decision Making at the Classroom Level

Stage Three: Reflection

- Brainstorm all the possible reasons why the situations described in the summary statements (Stage Two) could exist.
- Think deeply about how a change in practice might improve student achievement in this area.
- Then think about what learning is needed to be able to change practice.
- Be collaborative, says Richardson: talk with administrators, grade level colleagues, and/or mentors.
- This is the stage for self-confrontation. It is the stage, says Richardson, for "brutal honesty about strengths and weaknesses. Goal-setting will only be as good as the quality of reflection that precedes it."

Stage Four: Identify Goals

The data summaries evoke reflection on needs and the identified needs are translated into goal statements in much the same way as school goals are generated (as described in Workbook Two: *Creating a Process*).

Stage Five: Assemble Goals Into an Action Plan

- Writing goals is not enough; the goals must be translated into action steps.
- Break apart each goal and identify all the things that have to be done to achieve the goal. Out of all the available options, select which strategies would work best in the local situation and given the particular needs identified.
- Also identify necessary support mechanisms: action research, book clubs, study groups, peer observation/peer coaching, and so forth.
- Given that an essential part of a plan is to evaluate success in achieving the goals that are set, decide in advance how this will be done. What kind of progress will provide evidence of the goal being met? Have success criteria/ success indicators been established? What data sources will be used? Will student testing data be used? What else?

In the planning sheets included as Appendix C, Richardson describes a planning format very similar to the author's "1,4,5,2,3" action planning approach for school-level improvement described in Workbook Two: *Creating a Process*. Moreover, in adapting this approach for the teacher level, the author (2001) has suggested the following kind of planner.

PERSONAL CLASSROOM PROJECTS
In the light of your team's Action Plan, what emerges as an appropriate **Focus Area** for your personal classroom? What is your personal goal?
What is the **District and/or Building Goal** that your personal project addresses? What action steps are suggested to you from the original Action Plan?
Given your interest in this topic, what **external data** (regarding potential strategies to use) do you have available to you?
What **baseline data** do you have available to you to indicate the current status in your topic area?
What **strategies/interventions** are you going to use to achieve the desired results?
What **up-close data** do you plan to collect during implementation?

Data Profiles at the Teacher/Classroom Level
Task 6: Using a Classroom Action Planning Sheet

Purpose: To use the action planning sheet for personal classroom projects.

Grouping: Work on your own.

Directions: Working individually and using the "Personal Classroom Projects" worksheet shown above, create an action plan for one of your personal classroom projects.

Benefits of Learning Plans for Teachers

In the same edition of the National Staff Development Council's (NSDC's) *Tools For Schools* (February/March 2002) in which Joan Richardson's article appears, "Dr. Developer" has this to say about learning plans for teachers:

> When teachers don't have their own plans for growth, it's relatively easy for schools and districts to make decisions about staff development based on their perceived needs of a large group. The use of individual professional development plans has the potential to shift that power-equation substantially. With such plans in place, teachers can demonstrate their interest in certain types of learning—both in terms of the topics they believe will yield the greatest results and strategies that they believe will be most effective.
>
> The expectations for teachers are constantly changing, especially as standards-based instruction becomes more wide-spread. If teachers don't measure themselves against these standards, they will, quite simply, fall behind.
>
> Teachers are connected to a system. They are not independent contractors who can go into a room, close the door, and teach whatever and however they choose. They are accountable to other teachers, to their students, and to society in general in a way they never have been before. Because of that, the resources that are devoted to helping them improve their practice must be focused much more tightly than in years past.
>
> By developing your own professional learning plan, you will become a stronger, more influential advocate for your own learning—and, by example, for the learning that's beneficial to your colleagues and your students.

This important passage touches on four issues that are central, recurring themes in this workbook.

1. Through the use of such professional growth plans, teachers can put their personal stamp on their professional development activities. Such personalized, customized approaches are definitely needs-based data-driven.

2. The plans have dual strengths: they are focused on identified teacher needs, while, at the same time, aligned with school and district goals.

3. These focused plans are much more unlikely to lead to the frittering away of resources.

4. One of the real benefits of the four-level approach built into this workbook is the creation of a two-way street of disaggregation and aggregation. By means of the individual plans, data-based needs are identified for each teacher (disaggregation) and these needs and plans can then be put together (aggregation) and examined in order to design customized professional development programs that cater to the collective needs of participants. This same benefit works at the intersections of the other levels: individual student needs can be disaggregated and then aggregated for the entire class; teacher needs can be disaggregated and aggregated; and, at the school/district interface, needs are identified for each school and for the entire local system.

The Law of Reciprocal Data Use

This is the Law of Reciprocal Data Use at work. This law is a fundamental concept in the formation of the model presented in this workbook. The law is a simple one: it decrees that what is aggregated can always be disaggregated to inform the system level below and what is disaggregated can always be aggregated to inform the system level above, as shown in the following diagram.

The following is an example of this law at work at the student/class interface. Using a simple spreadsheet, a teacher can collate pertinent information about each student in terms of the three categories of data suggested by Fox (2001): Student Learning Outcome Data, Demographic Data, and Process Data, which include the instructional strategies and interventions already used with particular students and then go both ways with the data.

In the case of the spreadsheet illustrated below, each column would be further subdivided to include specific kinds of data. These specific data types are described in the pages following the spreadsheet.

MATRIX FOR CLASSROOM PROFILE

Sample for Elementary Reading

Student Name	Student Learning Outcome Data	Demographic Data	Process Data: Instructional Strategies/Interventions

The teacher can use this matrix to look for specific issues concerning individual students or groups of students (disaggregation) and common problems affecting the whole class (aggregation). According to Fox:

> **The skillful use of classroom data allows us to identify strengths and weaknesses in student learning, monitor student progress toward specified goals, make adjustments in instruction, measure the degree to which students meet standards, and distinguish between effective and ineffective instructional practice. Without data, instruction becomes a series of well-intentioned, but random, acts of teaching.**
>
> **At the heart of effective instruction is the skillful use of classroom data. They provide the teacher and administrator with the day-to-day feedback that is necessary for effective instructional decision-making. The first step in helping teachers and administrators work with data is to provide them with a conceptual model for thinking about data.**

Consequently, those in the Reading Success Network (RSN) in California use a model that distinguishes three kinds of data: outcome data, demographic data, and process data. Taken together, says Fox, the three kinds of data lead to the systematic, targeted, and purposeful instruction that results in high levels of student achievement.

Outcome Data

Outcome data indicate the degree to which an individual or group of students have demonstrated particular knowledge or skills and have achieved specified goals (or standards, benchmarks, objectives, or other learning targets). Outcome data distinguish teaching (process) from learning (product).

Sample Sources of Outcome Data

- Teacher-made tests
- Publishers' tests
- State-level tests
- Proficiency tests
- Report cards
- Exhibitions

- Portfolios
- Performance tasks
- National norm-referenced tests
- District-level tests
- Grade-level tests
- Projects
- Homework assignments
- Observations
- Graduation rate

Demographic Data

Demographic data refer to information regarding the student, his or her family, and community. These data also refer to the experiences, attitudes, and perceptions that affect the manner and rate in which students learn. Effective instructional decision making is made in the context of what is to be learned (outcome data) and to whom (demographic data). Viewed as an explanation (not an excuse), demographic data help teachers understand student performance and provide critical information for instruction.

The task is one of identifying the demographic factors that influence student learning, understanding how those factors affect learning, and using that information to design the most effective learning experiences for those particular students. Some of the factors to consider are: level of English language proficiency; experience in kindergarten and/or pre-school; the level of support provided at home; developmental level of students; special educational needs; and students' level of fluency in their primary language.

Sample Demographic Data

- Language proficiency
- Parent education level
- Gender
- Special program enrollment
- Attendance record
- Mobility/transiency

- Socio-economic status
- Family configuration
- Family support
- Parent language proficiency
- Community support services
- Student age
- Pre-school experience
- Discipline record
- Primary language fluency

Process Data

Process data are concerned with the components, practices, and strategies that comprise the instructional program in the classroom and at the school and district levels. They are the only data that teachers and administrators can control (as opposed to influence). Process data focus on the interventions and adjustments made in the instructional program to better cater to those students not making adequate progress. They are considered "change data," says Fox, as they relate to teacher and administrator behavior. Outcome and demographic data can be collected indefinitely, but nothing will change until process issues are addressed and there are changes made in teacher and administrator behavior. Such issues may include: the formative assessments used; the variety of instructional strategies; time allotted to direct instruction; time devoted to in-class practice; amount and nature of homework; differentiated instruction; curriculum organization; the materials used; grouping strategies, and so on.

Sample Process Data

- Curriculum organization
- Instructional time
- Textbooks
- Instructional strategies
- Special programs
- Equipment

- Assessment practices
- Staff mobility and attendance
- Interventions
- Supplemental materials
- Professional development opportunities
- Classroom management

Framing a Data Profile at the Teacher/Classroom Level

As covered in the previous chapter, when discussing using data profiles at the student level, Victoria Bernhardt has identified the same three categories of data as Dennis Fox (Student Learning Outcomes, Demographics, and Processes) but she also adds a fourth—Perceptions. In order to retain the integrity of the model posited in this workbook, it is important to use Bernhardt's frame once again, but, this time, in conjunction with the pioneering work of Charlotte Danielson and the framework for teaching. Indeed, by linking Bernhardt's four categories of data and Danielson's four domains of effective teaching in the form of a matrix, an interesting sixteen-cell data map emerges (as follows) that can be used to frame research questions, data collection and, indeed, the formation of a comprehensive Data Profile at the Teacher/Classroom Level.

DATA MAP FOR THE TEACHER/CLASSROOM LEVEL

	Indicators of Effective Teaching			
	Student Learning	**Demographics**	**Perceptions**	**Processes**
Planning and Preparation	**1** The Intended Curriculum —What to teach (tied to standards and benchmarks) —How to teach (instructional strategies) —How to assess (assessment methods) Intended Student Learning Outcomes	**2** Knowledge of students, their learning styles, and learning needs Knowledge of what works for which students	**3** Knowledge of how different groups of students feel about their learning Plans for involving and motivating these various groups	**4** Up-to-date knowledge of research-based instructional strategies Knowledge of resources
Learning Environment	**5** Creation of a disciplined learning environment Collaborative application of classroom rules	**6** Creation of a gender-friendly classroom atmosphere Racial diversity is honored and celebrated	**7** Creation of an inclusive classroom climate All students feel safe and respected	**8** Strategies are used to create a respectful, inclusive classroom climate Cooperative learning/needs-based grouping arrangements are utilized
Instruction	**9** The instructor teaches with standards and benchmarks always in mind The instructor aligns assessments with standards and benchmarks	**10** Differentiated instructional methods are used to maximize the learning of all students The teacher engages the students in their learning	**11** Students and parents feel that this is a caring and effective teacher Parents indicate that they know the grade level expectations	**12** The teacher selects the right instructional strategies and programs, i.e., those most likely to impact his/her students Instructional strategies are used effectively
Professional Responsibilities	**13** Student Learning Data are used to reflect on his/her teaching The teacher researches new instructional strategies	**14** The teacher studies the literature on how social and economic factors can affect student learning The teacher reflects on how to better support student sub-groups	**15** The teacher receives feedback from students, parents, colleagues, and mentors The teacher responds to the feedback	**16** The teacher establishes a Professional Growth Plan The teacher participates in relevant professional development opportunities and school/district projects

Data Profiles at the Teacher/Classroom Level
Task 7: Indicators of Effective Teaching

Purpose: To use the Indicators of Effective Teaching matrix to reflect on current instructional practice.

Grouping: Work on your own and then meet with your Learning Team.

Directions:

Step One: Focusing on your own practice, use the Indicators of Effective Teaching to identify five of your current strengths and five areas that are personal growth points. Record them in the space below.

Current Strengths	Growth Points
1.	1.
2.	2.
3.	3.
4.	4.
5.	5.

Step Two: Share your findings and see which items are common across your team.

Quality Criteria and Their Application

Reviewing these 16 indicators of effective teaching (largely drawn from the work of Danielson) brings us back to the importance of quality criteria and their application. According to Danielson and McGreal (2000):

> **The idea of a professional portfolio, assembled and presented as part of an evaluation system, has gained popularity in recent years. Indeed, such an effort can offer a significant vehicle for professional reflection on practice. However, before jumping into requiring a portfolio as part of an evaluation system, those designing the system should be very clear about the evaluative criteria for which they want the teachers to provide evidence, and to use those criteria when setting the specifications for the portfolio.**

Whether we're talking about the construction of a portfolio or a profile, the task remains the same: to identify the criteria/indicators of effective practice and then the sources of evidence that can be used to satisfy the requirements. Danielson and McGreal (2000) cite the following sources of information:

- Observation
- Planning documents such as unit plans and lesson plans
- Teacher self-assessments and structured reflections
- Analysis of student work
- Work samples
- Teacher artifacts, e. g., letters to parents
- Logs of professional development
- Student, parent, and colleague feedback

Noyce, Perda, and Traver (2000) see teachers as creators and users of data.

> **Teachers are essential members of a data-driven culture. Much quantitative information in schools derives directly from their work with students. Teachers, in turn, use the analysis of data to improve their practice....A teacher doesn't need to be a statistician to be data-driven. Simple calculations such as frequencies, averages, and percentages provide enough information to answer many important questions.**

The same authors provide the following list:

How Teachers Can Be Data Savvy

1. *Identify questions related to student performance.* You are likely to be most interested in information related to your classroom, but schoolwide, districtwide, or statewide patterns can also be informative.

2. *Identify data and gather necessary information.* Take into account demographic information, such as gender, race, eligibility for free or reduced lunch, and language spoken at home. Looking at student responses to individual test questions tells you things that you can't learn from a single test score.

3. *Examine and use data.* Look at student performance in focused areas to target particular groups for assistance. Examine data from previous years. Regardless of how convincing patterns look, do not jump to conclusions. Look beneath the surface and ask more questions.

4. *Ask useful questions.*

    - How does performance for individuals and groups relate to state standards?
    - Is there variation across content areas?
    - How does the performance compare with other like groups, such as among students, schools, districts, states, and across the nation?
    - Are there data trends over time?
    - Are there existing initiatives in the school, district, or classroom that might help improve student performance? On the basis of what evidence?
    - What are the implications for your instructional practices or for your curriculum?
    - Do your findings suggest that you need more professional development?
    - How might other stakeholders benefit from this information?

(Noyce, Perda, and Traver, 2000)

The Promise of Technology

Ernest Morgan (2001) has argued for the benefits of data management in the classroom using electronic means. Computerized databases and "standard" software packages, he says, can provide both organizational benefits (managing student data in the classroom) and reporting benefits (disseminating aggregate class data to administrators and parents). According to Morgan:

> **To begin with, you must identify your needs clearly and then the appropriate software, all the while remembering your chief goal is to manage your data needs so that you may free up time for the more important aspects of teaching.**

In the NAESP report, *Essentials for Principals: Data-Based Decision-Making* (2001), the promise of technology is seen as the ability to effectively collect, store, make sense of, and report on various aspects of an educational program in real time. Available tools, says the report, include: digital portfolios, computerized grade books, electronic lesson planners, and recent assessments with the scores charted in such a way as to aid analysis. Three crucial benefits of these approaches are mentioned. The technology provides the ability to

- maintain ongoing multi-dimensional portfolios of what students are learning, while managing the information in a way that is easily accessible
- allow teachers and administrators to look at performance over time and at several levels (individual student, classes, school wide, and district wide) and thus realize the promise of this workbook
- access proven resources from other educators

According to the same report, what can be accessed is tantamount to

> **...a living bank of proven, standards-referenced instructional materials, lessons, units, and assessments perfected through action research....The digital promise allows an online dialogue where teachers and schools can share concerns and successes. This forum allows the mentoring process to happen anytime, any place. Interaction can take place in a real time "chat," or through an email exchange. Or it can be structured as a discussion in the "forum." For the first time, teachers truly have the opportunity to collaborate on lessons and units with a wide range of fellow practitioners.**

In so doing, educators will be involved in electronic networking and will be meeting Elmore's (1996) challenge by sharing, pooling, and "getting to scale with good educational practice."

How technology-savvy are your teachers' portfolios?

The same NAESP report provides the following questions for educators to use as they reflect on their teachers' portfolios:

- How do you currently store assessment scores and artifacts? How accessible are audio, video, multimedia, and performance assessment materials?
- Do you have timely access to aggregated/disaggregated data for comparison purposes? How do you sort, organize, and display the data so that it facilitates analysis?
- How many times do you repeat the same data output—report card information, district and school forms, IEPs, lesson plans, or student study contracts?
- How can you streamline and organize anecdotal observations of student learning?
- How do you archive successful lesson plans, activities, and assessments? Is the majority of your professional library at home or at work?
- Do teachers, parents, and students have immediate access to multiple examples of student work and exemplary work samples?
- How do you manage the enormous amounts of data that schools are required to collect as well as the additional data the school wants to collect?
- Is accountability high on your priority list? Do you have your own copy of the standards for each subject area in your school? Do you reference them when planning, teaching, and learning?
- How do you manage the grading and reporting process?
- How and when do you collaborate with other educators? Look at student work? Share assessment practices and insights? Share professional dialogue? What's missing in your current method of storage and retrieval of data about student learning?

Data Profiles at the Teacher/Classroom Level
Task 8: Benefits of Technology

Purpose: To use the NAESP prompts to reflect on the promise of technology.

Grouping: Work on your own and then meet with your Learning Team.

Directions: On your own, review the NAESP list of reflective questions and ask each of these questions of your current practice. Identify six areas where the application of technology would have the greatest (beneficial) impact on your practice and record them below. Meet with your Learning Team to share these applications and discuss next steps to making them a reality, including prioritizing them and identifying the benefits and drawbacks of each area.

Beneficial Applications

In summary, at the classroom level, a Teacher Portfolio/Data Profile is

- a compilation of data relative to this particular teacher and his/her classroom, instruction, and students and their learning
- a working portfolio (literally a box by the teacher's desk say Danielson and McGreal, 2000) that can be condensed into a showcase document for presentation purposes
- the basis for personal (and team) deliberation, reflection, and decision making
- the springboard for professional growth planning
- the launch pad for diagnostic teaching and classroom interventions
- an ideal candidate for conversion to an electronic format
- the platform that enables classroom teachers to look both ways—internally and externally—on behalf of the students' learning and their instruction

By looking inward, both student learning and instructional needs are identified and, by looking outward, external expectations, standards, and quality criteria (for both students and teachers) are countenanced. The following simple chart can be used at the teacher/classroom level as an organizer of internal data (needs) and external data (expectations) concerning the students' learning and the teacher's instruction, leading to the identification of priorities for development for both the students (the class) and the teacher.

ORGANIZING AND PRIORITIZING DATA

	Internal Data (Needs)	External Data (Expectations)
Student Learning		
Instruction		

Data Profiles at the Teacher/Classroom Level
Task 9: Promoting EFFECTS at the Classroom Level

Purpose: To provide review questions to be asked of the teacher/classroom level.

Grouping: Work on your own and then meet with your Learning Team.

Directions: On your own, review this chapter and reflect on the following question: In what ways can teacher/classroom level data profiles promote each aspect of the EFFECTS model? Using the following chart, be as specific as possible as you link teacher/classroom level data profiles with the EFFECTS model. Meet with your Learning Team to share completed charts.

EFFECTS	Specific ways that teacher/classroom data profiles promote EFFECTS
Establishing clear expectations.	
Feedback being provided to the learners in progress reviews.	
Formatively screening for the purpose of diagnostic intervention.	
Examining, reflecting, and making decisions on the strength of the data.	
Committing to personal goals and growth plans.	
Taking responsibility for implementing and monitoring the plans.	
Summatively assessing progress toward desired learner outcomes.	

Notes

CHAPTER 4

CHAPTER FOUR: USING A DATA PROFILE AT THE SCHOOL LEVEL

As explored in Workbook Two: *Creating a Process*, data-based school improvement efforts continue to unfold in schools across the nation. Indeed, the *No Child Left Behind* Act provides further impetus for these activities. Moreover, there is increasing evidence that these efforts are paying off in terms of increased levels of student achievement.

The Louisiana Staff Development Council (LSDC) has recently published one example of such a success story (see Richardson, 2003). A research team visited twelve schools considered "academically above average," according to the Louisiana Accountability System, with at least 80 percent of their students living in poverty. According to Richardson (2003), the LSDC investigators identified seven characteristics that were consistently present in each of the twelve high poverty, high performing schools, as follow:

Louisiana Study: High Poverty, High Performing School

Seven characteristics present in each of the twelve "Can Do" schools visited:

1. Each school used many types of job-embedded staff development—coaching, mentoring, examination of and reflection on student work and instructional practices, visitation to other classrooms and other schools, conferences, workshops, serving on curriculum committees, and so on. Less common was the use of case studies or action research in a formal sense.

2. The principal and staff had a strong sense of efficacy—they believed in the power of teaching and in their own ability to ensure that every student learns, regardless of obstacles.

3. In every school, the primary job responsibility of at least one individual (often the principal) was to oversee instruction and know what was going on in the classrooms. Although an instructional leader guided the learning process for teachers and provided the necessary resources, each of the twelve schools was a true "community of learners" where faculty collaboration was considered critical to improved practice.

4. Analyzing student data was the first step and the driving force in the professional learning process. The schools analyzed data, especially looking at test results, to identify areas of broad, common needs and each student's specific strengths and weaknesses.

5. Teachers tried different approaches to meet student needs—grouping and structuring, use of materials, a variety of instructional strategies—always with an eye toward continuous assessment.

Continued

6. Standards-based instruction was pervasive and teachers could readily discuss how the lessons matched content standards.

7. All schools had excellent school-wide discipline characterized by a shared sense of responsibility for all students. There was a general understanding that children of poverty often come from homes without a great deal of structure or academic support. Structured classroom procedures and high expectations were considered the foundation for success.

(Richardson, 2003)

What stands out in these schools is that, in putting the improvement of student learning before everything else, their work begins with data. They begin with a thorough analysis of student data (as in the Pella case study described earlier in this workbook), which points them in the direction of student and adult needs, school-wide goals, and more focused professional development activities. Indeed, analyzing student data is described as the first step and the driving force in the professional learning process. Moreover, the data (especially test results) are analyzed on two levels: to identify areas of broad, common needs and, within those, each student's personal strengths and weaknesses. In one of the schools studied, Richardson (2003) reports teachers analyzed disaggregated test data to identify weaknesses in grade groups and for each individual child on each teacher's roster for the fall, while, in another school, a similar analysis resulted in an IEP-type plan for each student. Folded within school-level data, needs, goals, and plans, therefore, are teacher needs, goals, and plans, and individual and groups of students' needs, goals, and plans.

A Data Profile at the School Level
Task 1: Progress Review

Purpose: To use the LSDC checklist as a progress review.

Grouping: Work on your own and then meet with your Learning Team.

Directions: Rate your school on each of the seven characteristics identified in the LSDC list using a 5-point scale where 1 = "No Evidence" up to 5 = "Considerable Evidence." Share and discuss your ratings with your Learning Team.

School Rating	Characteristic
_______	1. Job-embedded staff development activities support the professional learning of staff members.
_______	2. The principal and staff have a strong sense of efficacy and believe they can significantly impact the academic achievement of all students.
_______	3. Instructional leadership is combined with staff collaboration to produce a true "community of learners."
_______	4. Student data is analyzed to identify whole school needs and goals and specific strengths and weaknesses of individual students.
_______	5. Teachers use multiple strategies to meet students' needs and to support continuous growth in their learning.
_______	6. Standards-based instruction and assessment are widely practiced.
_______	7. There is excellent school-wide discipline characterized by a shared sense of responsibility for all students.

Steps to Success

What are some of the other data-related building blocks that can be put in place to ensure the same level of success as that achieved in the schools in the Louisiana study? In reading case study material about other successful sites, it is clear that various activities can be used as catalysts for data-driven school improvement efforts:

- Some schools hold annual data retreats.
- Some schools issue a regular stream of data-based "mini-progress reports" put together by their designated data analysts/data coaches.
- Some schools use professional development sessions to study disaggregated data and plan targeted interventions.
- Some schools compile Data Profiles/School Portfolios to store the accumulating data and from which to extract need analyses and reports when required.
- Some schools do all, or a combination of the activities, listed above.

Data Retreats

According to Alison Cromey (2001), Data Retreats are a conduit for change in schools. They can be used to lead teams of educators (and, in some cases, members of other stakeholder groups) through reflective collaboration and illumination about their school's data, resulting in the creation of data-driven school improvement plans.

A data retreat provides the time, place, and guidance for team members to come together for a few days, work through various types of data, and develop their own data-based goals and action plans (Cromey, 2001).

Data retreats, then, provide a time-bound forum for completing several of the stages of the process of continuous school improvement as described in Workbook Two: *Creating a Process*. Training materials from the North Central Regional Educational Laboratory (NCREL) lay out eight steps in the data retreat process:

Stage One: Before the Retreat

1. Develop a school improvement team.
2. Collect and organize data.

Stage Two: During the Retreat

3. Analyze data and define needs.
4. Generate hypotheses.
5. Set improvement goals.
6. Identify specific strategies.
7. Define evaluation criteria.
8. Make a commitment to: implementing specific strategies; applying criteria to evaluate the attainment of goals; and adjusting strategies as necessary.

According to the same NCREL materials, data retreats provide training that is

- relevant: participants work with their own data
- constructivist: those involved, by interpreting the data, establish their own meaning

- collaborative: educators work in teams to make sense of the data and build intervention plans around the identified needs
- reflective: participants commit to the thoughtful, insightful study of their data
- productive: meaningful school improvement plans are created in which the participants have ownership and investment
- capacity-building: by working intensively with colleagues, school and district leaders improve their own leadership capacity

  By doing school improvement in these data retreats, they are better able to do school improvement efforts in the future. Indeed, echoing Elmore's (2000) concept of distributed leadership, it cannot be emphasized enough how important a role that **teacher leaders** (who may or may not be part of the formal leadership structures of their schools) play in data-driven school improvement activities.

- comprehensive: patterns are uncovered by using four lenses of data—student achievement, demographic, program, and perceptions

Data Analysts

As previously noted, Killion and Bellamy (2000) recommend the deployment of trained data analysts at the school level. While school-based data analysts do not replace the need for district research and evaluation specialists (school-based data analysts depend on a flow of accurate and well-organized district and state data to be able to perform their work), they do take the use of data a step further.

> School-based data analysts use district and state data sources, and go beyond them to identify particular patterns in their school's achievement. For most school-based data analysts, being able to identify the strengths and weaknesses in student knowledge and skills is the core of their role....Another aspect of data analysts' work is organizing data that already exist in files and reports, but which are mostly unusable because they are discrete or unknown. **Data analysts compile school portfolios that include multiple indicators of a school's performance.** When the data are compiled in one place and organized in formats that are easy to understand, they are accessible and useful to those making decisions (Killion and Bellamy, 2000).

There are three important implications arising from this passage.

1. One of the important roles of school-based data analysts is to provide their colleagues with regular reports concerning the progress of student achievement. Such focused reports, says Schmoker (2003), can address two central questions:

   - How many students (and which) are succeeding in the subjects I teach?
   - Within these same subjects, what are the areas of strength or weakness?

   Armed with the answers to these questions, colleagues can then mount instructional interventions and improvements in the identified deficit areas, followed by the ongoing collection of formative assessment data—gathered every few weeks—that enable team members to gauge the levels of success and to adjust their instructional efforts accordingly. Such an approach, says Schmoker (2003), adds simplicity and economy to the school improvement process and results in targeted, focused change efforts.

2. Data analysts, in attending to the "multiple indicators of a school's performance," would do well to use the eleven factors (the "primary determinants of student achievement") recently identified by Robert Marzano (2003), as follow:

Primary Determinants of Student Achievement

School-Level Factors

a. A guaranteed and viable curriculum with certain content being addressed in an adequate amount of time.

b. Challenging goals and effective feedback. Assessment data are used—at least once every nine weeks—to set specific learning goals for individual students and to monitor progress toward those goals.

c. Parent and community involvement.

d. A safe and orderly environment.

e. Staff collegiality and professionalism involving a rigorous and comprehensive professional development program that encourages teachers to try new instructional strategies in an action research mode.

Teacher-Level Factors

f. A repertoire of highly effective instructional strategies is utilized that can be adapted for use with different students with different needs.

g. Classroom management, including the use of disciplinary interventions that are applied in the context of appropriate teacher-student relationships.

h. Classroom curriculum design that involves the appropriate sequencing and pacing of learning tasks.

Student-Level Factors

i. Home atmosphere that is supportive of the student and his/her academic achievement.

j. Learned intelligence and background knowledge, including a wealth of incidental learning.

k. Student motivation and interest in learning.

(Marzano, 2003)

3. Killion and Bellamy (2000) maintain that school-based data analysts bring together various kinds of data in School Portfolios that can then be used as the basis for their regular, ongoing reports to colleagues and for dialogue and analysis during data retreats and other kinds of data-using sessions.

A Data Profile at the School Level
Task 2: Data Retreats and Data Analysts

Purpose: To have an opportunity to respond to what has been learned about data retreats and data analysts.

LT

Grouping: Work with your Learning Team.

Directions: In your team, reflect on the following two questions:

What are you doing already that is similar to data retreats and the work of data analysts?

From what you have read about data retreats and data analysts, how could this work be strengthened?

School Portfolios

Victoria Bernhardt has done more than anyone else to popularize the idea of compiling and using a School Portfolio (Bernhardt, 1994). The context for establishing a School Portfolio, she says, is continuous improvement and data-based decision making in schools. Indeed, she describes the context as follows:

> For real and appropriate changes to be implemented, staffs within a school must conduct comprehensive needs analyses of students, teachers, and the school community; develop a shared vision, based on the values and beliefs, and personal visions of the individuals in the school community; and establish a governance structure to support the bottom-up approach. Then, utilizing this information, they must develop a comprehensive action plan to increase teachers' repertoire of skills and understanding; include the community as true partners; evaluate the impact of new strategies; and establish a plan for continuous improvement.

As at the other system levels, this process of continuous improvement (which, for the school level, is more fully described in Workbook Two: *Creating a Process*) is informed by the information contained in a Data Profile. To Bernhardt, however, the idea of a School Portfolio embraces not only such a data base but also all the other documentation put together to trigger school improvement. Her definition of a School Portfolio is as follows:

> A school portfolio is a purposeful collection of work telling the story of the school. A school portfolio describes efforts to engender and maintain systemic and continuous school improvement and exhibits the school goals, vision, plans, and progress. **A school portfolio allows for the continuous collection and assessment of evidence and is always evolving, growing, improving, and enabling schools to make better decisions.**

In arguing that "a comprehensive school portfolio provides a uniquely appropriate and effective framework for describing current processes, and for planning, monitoring, and evaluating school improvement efforts," Bernhardt is echoing what has been said about the role of portfolios/data profiles at the other system levels, but is now focused on the school/organizational level. Indeed, she maintains that such a portfolio/data profile should possess characteristics common to the "measurements" used to create successful business organizations as defined by Tom Peters in *Thriving on Chaos* (1987). The School Portfolio should

- have a simple presentation and be easy to read and understand
  It should contain text, graphs, and charts and a hard copy should be available for viewing by all interested parties at any time.

- contain visible measurements (quality criteria/benchmarks), developed or adapted by staff
- be the result of everyone's efforts
  As many colleagues as possible should be involved in its design, development, and maintenance.
- include an undistorted collection of primary information, such as student achievement and demographic data over several years
- adopt a straightforward measurement approach which, in Bernhardt's case, involves a combination of rubrics and outcome indicators
- be accompanied by an overall sense of urgency and perpetual improvement, which results from identifying and acknowledging discrepancies between where the school is and where the school wants to be

Bernhardt (1994) also lists the purposes and uses of a School Portfolio. It provides the opportunity to do the following:

- Establish one document that describes an overall school plan, and the school's mission, vision, beliefs, and rationale for improvement.
- Document efforts on a number of elements important to school improvement.
- Understand the complexities of the school as an organization, including the interrelationships between the various elements.
- Provide readily accessible and necessary information for data-based decision making. A comprehensive school portfolio, says Bernhardt, includes data about the school—its population, facilities, resources, test scores, the results of self-assessments, and so forth.
- Reflect on the progress made. Reminding colleagues of where we were when we started and how far we've traveled since then can be extremely motivational for those involved. Colleagues, says Bernhardt, are much more willing to work hard if they see the benefits of their hard work.
- Troubleshoot the continuous improvement efforts of the school and identify areas for interventions based on diagnostic information.

The school portfolio visually chronicles the progress (or lack of progress) made in each element of the school improvement process in text, graphs, charts, and pictures. This information helps a school staff decide where to focus efforts needed to increase the effectiveness of their actions. Additionally, the school

> portfolio can be used to identify elements incongruent with the school's vision, mission, outcomes, and plan—which deter the progress of the school's improvement efforts (Bernhardt, 1994).

- (Self-) assess and guide the school's unique approach to continuous improvement against established criteria.
- Be accountable.
- Communicate with all local stakeholder groups and potential partners. According to Bernhardt, those organizations that do a good job of communication with the wider school community tend to receive external support in due measure.

  A comprehensive school portfolio effectively serves as a public record to communicate important information about the school, its purpose, mission, and vision, the values and beliefs held by staff, its plans for improvement, the reasons particular approaches have been chosen, and the results of the school improvement efforts.
- Replace or provide the wherewithal for a local, state, or regional accreditation process.

In summary, says Bernhardt:

> Because school improvement is an ongoing, complex, and multifaceted process, the portfolio is the most appropriate and authentic means to chronicle the multidimensionality of school improvement and its development over time. Schools that use a school portfolio benefit immensely from ownership and a shared meaning of the improvement process and its results. A school portfolio, combined with assessment criteria, allows for a deep understanding of the elements and processes of a school, what needs to be improved and why, how the school plans to carry out the improvement efforts, the expected outcomes of the approach to improvement, the efforts to implement the plan, and the results of the effort. A school portfolio provides a view of the big picture of all the elements and shows how they interrelate to make a whole. With a school portfolio, it is easy to see what needs to be altered to keep the efforts progressing.... **A comprehensive school portfolio is an excellent organizer of all information necessary to make informed decisions about any part or all parts of a school.**

A Data Profile at the School Level
Task 3: Benefits of Compiling a School Portfolio

Purpose: To digest the work of Bernhardt and to reflect on its application.

LT

Grouping: Work in pairs and then meet with your Learning Team.

Directions: Based on your reading of what Victoria Bernhardt has to say about school portfolios, develop the arguments that you could use to convince your colleagues that compiling a school portfolio is an important school improvement activity. In addition, try to anticipate colleagues' possible resistance to or concerns about the idea. Share your arguments with your Learning Team and discuss how colleague resistance/concerns might be resolved. Use the space provided below for note taking.

Benefits of a School Portfolio

Possible resistance or concerns

Success Criteria and Data Collection

Bernhardt (1994) says that both these elements—success criteria and data collection—should be contained in a School Portfolio. The success criteria can be self-created, adopted "off the shelf" (such as Marzano's [2003] list of "Primary Determinants of Student Achievement" included earlier in this chapter), or adapted from an existing statement. Whichever approach is finally selected, in terms of **guidelines for criteria**, Bernhardt provides this advice. They should be

- focused on what is important—student learning and student achievement
- simple to use
- indicative of what needs to happen in order to be successful
- clearly stated
- applicable for self-assessment
- challenging, but achievable—thereby effecting real improvement
- a working contract, as opposed to a form-driven exercise, that encourages ongoing conversation about what is important
- comprehensive in scope

Bernhardt (1994) incorporates success criteria into seven continua/rubrics that focus on key components of school improvement: information and analysis, leadership, student achievement, quality planning, professional development, partnership development, and continuous improvement and evaluation. Using these self-assessment rubrics, faculty members can plot the growth of their school over time in these seven major areas.

A Data Profile at the School Level
Task 4: Success Criteria for School Improvement

Purpose: To reflect on the importance of success criteria for school improvement.

Grouping: Work with your Learning Team.

Group process strategy: First work in pairs; then have pairs share with pairs. Come back together as a whole group and share key ideas developed in small-group work using the Tambourine strategy (see the **Group Process Guide**).

Directions: Use the following question as a prompt for small-group, followed by whole-group discussion:

Why is it always important to have success criteria for our school improvement efforts? Should any other criteria be considered and why?

Reasons for using success criteria for school improvement efforts

The Role of Data

As explained in previous workbooks, it is data that enable us to describe the status and extent of our current efforts—relative to the success criteria—and provide the wherewithal for conducting a gap analysis between where we are and where we want to be. In order to reinforce and substantiate the rubric-based self-assessment efforts, therefore, Bernhardt (1994) encourages schools to analyze existing data and collect—and analyze additional data when appropriate—in order to understand:

- current and future needs of the school, students, parents, teachers, and community

- how well the current processes meet the needs of these clients
- ways in which the school and community are changing
- root causes of problems
- types of educational programs and expertise that will be needed in the future

It is in this context that Bernhardt recommends studying four kinds of data: demographic data, perceptions data, student achievement data, and assessments of current and desired practices and processes. Taken together, these four kinds of data provide the information-base for school improvement. Consequently, says Bernhardt:

> **A positive, nonthreatening, ongoing monitoring system, such as a school portfolio, coupled with a measurement device, enables a school to move beyond adopting (as opposed to implementing) innovations and/or new strategies. When properly used, the portfolio approach helps to create and maintain a shared vision, and leads to the successful creation of a comprehensive learning organization.**

In terms of logistics, Bernhardt (1994) explains, there are a number of decisions to make regarding the following questions:

- Where will the portfolio be located and stored? (Bernhardt suggests using a binder with dividers.)
- Who will be the manager?
- What kinds of criteria will be used for monitoring progress?
- What kinds of baseline data will be used?
- In terms of a systematic management system, what goes into the portfolio and when?
- When and how will information be gathered and organized?
- What actions have to be taken and on what timelines?

Bernhardt also recommends not only the writing of a narrative that tells the story of the school, its vision, and its progress toward that vision, but also the updating of the portfolio on a regular basis with some material being shed and other contents being condensed.

A Data Profile at the School Level
Task 5: Considering the Logistics

Purpose: To discuss the logistics of compiling, maintaining, and using a school portfolio.

Grouping: Work on your own and then meet with your Learning Team.

Directions: Based on Victoria Bernhardt's comments, list the logistical considerations that have to be taken into account when compiling, maintaining, and using a school portfolio. Share and discuss these considerations with your Learning Team.

Logistical considerations:

Edie Holcomb on School Portfolios

Edie Holcomb (1999) describes how data are used to create alignment throughout the school improvement process. What are required initially are baseline data, but the school portfolio (as she also prefers to call it) continually expands as more data are acquired and used throughout the continuous improvement cycle. Holcomb explains:

> **When most schools make the commitment to become more data-driven, they are panic-stricken about where they are going to find information to include. Then they discover that there are "mother lodes" of data scattered throughout the school and district that have been as shrouded with mystery as the lost ark and certainly have never been mined. Once people begin to discover what they could include in the initial school portfolio, it becomes a challenge to limit its size and scope. [It is essential to**

> focus] the baseline school portfolio....The school portfolio is a work in progress at all times, and there will be ample opportunities to add more information or more detailed analysis as the process continues.

Indeed, Holcomb lists some of the data uses that take those involved beyond the baseline stage and the kinds of data that can be added to the portfolio over time.

- Data are one of the filters used to help the school focus on a limited number of top priority goals. "This is a critical point," she says, "because it establishes the awareness that the school portfolio was not just something 'finished and done with' but something that will be used regularly whenever decisions are pending."
- It is always important, she says, to study before taking action. What are required, says Holcomb, include

> ...further analysis of the issue or need, investigation of research and best practice, and improvement of assessment literacy. All of these involve data. Analysis of the existing situation may include further analysis of existing data or collection of additional data...this data becomes part of the school portfolio as it is continually updated....When new strategies are being selected, data that substantiate their claims of effectiveness should be a prerequisite. Deciding and learning how to assess attainment of the goals is learning how to amass data needed to document progress.

- Another task is to design the data collection for monitoring and evaluating the changes over time. Again, according to Holcomb:

> As improvement goals are crafted into language that will motivate whole-school effort, the question, "How will we know we're getting there?" should be addressed. Some answers will be very evident, because there are data sources that were already available and were used in the initial school portfolio that can be monitored over time. Standardized tests and state assessments are two examples. Other answers will have to be constructed as professionals discuss what could be measured, observed, or aggregated from information they already keep as individual teachers.
>
> Data collection [also has to occur] as implementation takes place. This may be of two types. Assessments have already been

> **identified for use when monitoring student performance. It may also be wise to collect data that verify the use of selected strategies. As these data are collected, they are added to the school portfolio, creating a stronger database for the next round of analysis, goal setting, and improvement.**

In the passage quoted above, Holcomb (1999) underscores three themes running throughout the PATHWISE *Data-Driven School Improvement Series*:

1. Data-based needs help us focus, target, and prioritize our school improvement efforts.
2. Data are added to the School Portfolio/Profile cumulatively over time.
3. Data accompany and drive the whole process of continuous school improvement.

She also touches on a major component of the four-level model explored in this workbook. Data have to be owned by those at each level—through participation in shared decision making and the actual gathering and analysis of data—to inform those same decisions. As Holcomb (1999) asserts:

> I prefer to talk about ownership, not as something purchased, but as something grown, crafted, or invented. You can "buy" something in a day, but you can only grow, craft, or invent something over time. **Ownership must be created along the way through involvement and communication at every step.**

Ownership of both the process and products of school improvement has to be nurtured, generated, and earned the hard way through ongoing involvement and dialogue. Data and the messages contained within them have to be "ours," thus strengthening our resolve to do something about them. And it's the same for students, teachers (individually and working together collectively as the school faculty), and the district leadership.

This issue of ownership is pertinent for two reasons: a) it cannot be by-passed, and b) most initiatives that encourage us to collect data come to schools from the outside making the internal generation of ownership and commitment even more important. The assembling of data in response to a set of external requirements—which will be increased exponentially by the requirements of *No Child Left Behind*—is what Holcomb (1999) calls the compliance approach. Such guidelines, she says, are available from a variety of sources, including accreditation organizations, recognition programs, and state mandates.

Holcomb provides an example of each of these external avenues to data collection as follows:

The NCA Way

As mentioned in Workbook Two: *Creating a Process*, the North Central Association of Colleges and Schools (NCA) requires schools and school districts to develop a School Profile as part of its accreditation and endorsement processes. In the NCA handbook, *Developing the School Profile* (NCA personnel evidently prefer to use the term "Profile"), published in 2000, besides the School and Community and School Mission Statement, several kinds of data are called for:

- Unique local insights
- Information about the success of former students
- Available data on students, school, and community characteristics
- Student characteristics:
    - standardized tests
    - entrance examination results
    - readiness tests
    - other common (every-student) measures
- Instructional data
- Community data

Referring to the NCA stipulations, Holcomb (1999) makes these comments:

> Community needs assessments and climate surveys are used to provide insights on the unique nature of the local context for schooling. Information on former students includes typical graduate follow-up studies, focus groups and interviews with students who have moved from elementary to middle school to high school, and feedback from dropouts. Sometimes feedback from universities and employers can also be obtained.
>
> Typical data on students include enrollment, attendance, suspensions and expulsions, dropout rate, standardized test scores, ACT and SAT participation and scores, mobility, and co-curricular participation. These data are disaggregated to

compare performance of various groups within the student population.

Schools seem to have more difficulty compiling instructional data, and usually include staff development participation and surveys of most common instructional techniques. This is the appropriate place for information about what the school provides in the ways of programs and opportunities.

Community data may include a description of local, state, and federal mandates that affect the school or demographic information on population trends, income, and employment.

Blue Ribbon Criteria

The second example of Holcomb's compliance approach is the U. S. Department of Education's recognition program known as National Schools of Excellence and Blue Ribbon Schools. As a participant in this process since 1991, Holcomb attests to its increasing emphasis on assessment and documentation of results in student learning. In providing complete answers to questions in the 1997 nomination form for high schools, participating sites needed to provide the following kinds of data:

Demographic Data

- Enrollment by grade level
- Per pupil expenditure
- Racial/ethnic composition
- Student mobility rate
- Percentage of limited English proficient students
- Percentage of students qualifying for free or reduced-price lunches
- Percentage of students receiving special education services

Student Data

- Student participation rates in nonacademic services and programs
- Student participation in co-curricular activities and the degree to which it is representative of the overall composition of the student body
- Percentage of students who exceed graduation requirements

Data on Teaching and Learning

- Usage data from library, information, and media services
- Number of students moving among ability groups, especially into groups with more challenging course work
- Participation in professional development and evidence of impact on improved teaching
- Evidence of how analysis of data at the school level has resulted in specific improvements
- Evidence of how technology has contributed to increased use of data for decision making

Data on School, Family, and Community Partnerships

- Data on family involvement in school activities and the degree to which the families involved are representative of the overall student body

Indicators of Success

- Results of standardized tests for each of the last five years, disaggregated according to the largest and most significant subgroups in the school
- Results of non-standardized, or alternative, assessments developed at the school level
- Results of college entrance examinations (PSAT, SAT, ACT) and percentage of students tested
- Percentages of students in various educational and employment categories a year following graduation
- Daily student attendance
- Student dropout rate
- Daily teacher attendance
- Teacher turnover rate
- Results of climate surveys
- Percentages of students involved in various types of safety, discipline, and drug issues

State Laws

Prior to *No Child Left Behind*, many states had already instituted statewide data requirements for schools and school districts. As Holcomb (1999) comments, like many state education agencies, Wisconsin's Department of Public Instruction collects data regarding indicators of quality that are required by state law to be reported to the community each year. These include:

- Scores on Wisconsin's Reading Comprehension Test (Grade 3)
- Scores on Wisconsin Student Assessment System—Knowledge and Concepts examinations (Grades 4, 8, and 10)
- ACT results
- Advanced Placement testing
- Advanced course work
- Graduation requirements
- Graduation rates
- Postgraduation follow-up information
- Extracurricular and/or co-curricular activities
- Attendance
- Out-of-school suspensions
- Expulsions
- Retentions
- Dropouts
- Habitual truants
- Staffing ratios
- Revenues and expenditures

According to Holcomb (1999), this list can be a starting point as it identifies the kind of data readily available in most school districts. On the other hand, she says, there are several important distinctions between a state performance report like this and a school portfolio.

1. The most obvious one is the difference between a mandated list and a collection of data chosen by the members of a school faculty as having some significance for them.

2. The second distinction is that states are interested in district information and the school portfolio is focused on the individual building. If a district is large enough to have more than one school at any level (elementary, middle, or high school), the district's data will need to be broken down building by building.

3. The third difference is that the state reports are primarily quantitative, whereas school portfolios should include a balance of quantitative and qualitative data to reflect perceptions of staff, students, and constituents and to reap the benefits of data triangulation (see Workbooks Three: *Engaging in Action Research* and Four: *Analyzing and Understanding Data*).

4. Perhaps the most important contrast, however, is the type of comparisons made. State reports are used to compare districts throughout the state. A school portfolio would aim to include two different types of comparisons. One is a comparison of the school's own performance over time. The other would consist of comparisons with schools that are similar in nature and that achieve the desired results. As Holcomb (1999) explains:

> **This is *benchmarking*, as the term is used in the business sector. A business asks, "Who's in the same kind of business we are with the same kind of product trying to reach the same market—and doing it best?" A school might ask, "Who works with a similar student population in a similar context and has high achievement?" These comparisons help identify models for further study and can lead to networking with other schools.**

Holcomb (1999) concludes that, while one advantage of the compliance approach is that it is more efficient, one disadvantage is that it's more difficult to create sufficient ownership and commitment at the school level. Her solution to this problem of low interest on the part of those local to the situation is for them to start by generating a few key questions to get people engaged and then "slide" the data that's of local interest under the headings required by their state or district model.

This is the same concept introduced in Workbook Two: *Creating a Process*. The term used for it in Workbook Two was "docking"—as when spacecraft come together and interlock. The author's advice is the same as Edie Holcomb's: in order to deal with the "externality" of outside demands and requirements from a local perspective, take the given goal areas and create sub-goals that speak to the local data and local needs. As Holcomb says, it is this local flavor to which those in the school are committed—especially if they helped to collect and analyze the data and identify the emerging needs.

This issue of ownership and commitment is a by-product of the Law of Reciprocal Data Use. Individual students are much more likely to have interest in class-level data when it is disaggregated for them personally. By the same token, individual teachers are going to feel the same way about school-level data and those in a school about district-level data. Personalized data are what matters to people at whatever level of the system. Data Profiles and Portfolios can capture this same spirit. What is in a Student Profile is a student's data disaggregated for him/her and what is in a School Profile is the staff's data disaggregated for them. In general, the ownership lies at the level of decision making that is closest to the task at hand—Doyle's concept of subsidiarity (2002).

A Data Profile at the School Level
Task 6: Resolving Tensions

Purpose: To discuss the crucial issue of generating internal commitment to externally-generated, compliance-driven approaches.

LT

Grouping: Work with your Learning Team.

Directions: Use the following question as a prompt to explore the role of school portfolios:

What is there about a school portfolio that enables educators to use it in resolving the tension between external mandates and internal commitments?

Practical Purposes of the School Profile

Bellamy, Holly, and Sinisi (1997) introduced the concept of a School-Community Profile as follows:

> **The school-community profile is a summary description of the students and faculty within a specific school and the community characteristics that are relevant to student achievement and school improvement. The school-community profile provides a picture of what is taking place in the school and community that affects teaching and learning. School profiles are as varied as the schools they describe.**

> **The profile is usually a printed document compiled from the district's student information system and other sources. It is always a working document because data on students, the school, and the community are constantly changing. Additions and revisions are made as new information becomes available.**

According to the same authors, the school-community profile is important because it fulfills several practical purposes.

> **The school-community profile provides the information to understand the challenges facing the school and its students and to make plans for improvement....This helps the school respond to the unique circumstances of its community, teachers, students, and parents. By developing and maintaining a thorough profile, the school always has data available to keep the school community informed and to use for mandated local, state, and federal reporting.**

Holly and Lange (2002) expanded on these points when they compiled their *Practical Purposes of the School Profile*. A School Profile can be used for:

- Reporting to the district
- Comparing with other schools both in the district and other districts
- Developing needs assessments and different points in time
- Compiling annual progress reports for the state department
- Writing grant applications
- Reporting to parents and the community
- Writing comprehensive school improvement plans
- Writing a school brochure
- Sharing with prospective employees
- Sharing with visitors/prospective students and their parents

In Iowa, as in other states, schools and school districts have had to provide Annual Progress Reviews (APRs) and five-year Comprehensive School Improvement Plans (CSIPs) to the state department—even prior to the onset of *No Child Left Behind* and the need to demonstrate Annual Yearly Progress (AYP). In order to meet these requirements,

School Profiles have become one of the main vehicles for storing, condensing, and reporting on their data. The same School Profiles are also used for NCA accreditation work and at least one school, Irving Elementary in Dubuque, used its School Profile in its successful bid for Blue Ribbon recognition. When training school and district teams in how to compile School Profiles, Holly and Lange (2002) have always tried to incorporate the excellent advice given to schools by the North Central Association (NCA) in their accreditation handbooks.

A Data Profile at the School Level
Task 7: Meeting the Requirements of *No Child Left Behind*

Purpose: To reflect on the importance of having a school profile/school portfolio in meeting the requirements of *No Child Left Behind*.

Grouping: Work with your Learning Team. Select a recorder.

Group process strategy: Use a brainstorming strategy and create a team list.

Directions: Having a school profile/school portfolio is crucial in meeting the requirements of *No Child Left Behind*. As a team, brainstorm the reasons why this is the case. Try to be specific. Have your recorder make a list of the reasons. Use the space below for note taking.

The role of school portfolios in meeting the requirements of *NCLB*:

The School Profile: the NCA Advice

According to the NCA guidance materials (2000):

> The school profile is a concise stand-alone document developed to summarize information that describes the students within a specific school. To be useful the focus must be on community, student, and instructional characteristics that are relevant to student performance and school improvement.
>
> The profile enables the community to identify student strengths and needs. It is the document from which student performance goals emerge. As such, the profile provides baseline information relative to student performance that can be used later for comparisons when determining the success of the school's improvement plan.
>
> This stand-alone document should have the following characteristics:
>
> - Relatively brief—not pages of data.
> - Appropriate analysis of data—not lengthy descriptions of data.
> - Data that are important to know versus data that are nice to know.
> - Data developed and presented to be understood by the average person.
> - Data presented in charts, graphs, and other pictorial representations.
> - Succinct analysis of data to provide interpretations of findings. (What do these data mean?)
>
> The school profile is written by faculty members for faculty members. Information needs to be displayed in a format that will be readily usable by faculty members. Therefore, all parts of the profile should be shared and discussed by faculty. The goal of the document is to provide a picture of what is taking place in the school in terms of teaching and learning.

While agreeing that the school faculty is the first audience for the profile, there will be other audiences that will need to see the data summaries. There are two issues here. One is the need to preserve the faculty's right to be the first audience. As Holcomb (1999) has explained:

> **The only role group whose members are or may feel they are "lifers" are the school's staff, especially the teachers. Although the entire school improvement process should be participatory and decision-making should be shared, teachers must be given special status in the actual gathering and analysis of data.... [There are] several reasons why this is new, unfamiliar, uncomfortable work. Leaders should be sensitive to these feelings and provide shelter for teachers—not to shield them from the data, but to provide a safe environment for their explorations.**

All constituents have a right of access to data, but teachers should have first chance to explore and analyze and prepare to discuss it with others.

By constituents, Holcomb means interested adults outside the school, including parents and community members, who should be the second audience to receive the distilled information.

The second issue, however, concerns the communicability of the contents of the School Profile. As the data are prepared for other audiences, this issue becomes increasingly important. The crux of the matter is how to display the data. Again, the NCA provides good advice on this matter:

> As pieces are prepared for the profile they should contain two parts: graphics and highlights (text). Whenever possible, carefully constructed graphical displays which supplement text are preferable. Information that is presented in graphs, charts, and tables is understood more easily and quickly than are pages of text. Every visual display should be accompanied by a short, concise highlight statement providing an analysis of the data.
>
> Data Displays
>
> - Are simple.
>   They should be easily understood by all stakeholders.
> - Should be neat in appearance.
>   No more than two graphic displays per page.
>   One graphic display per page is ideal.
> - Should be complete enough to stand-alone.
>
> Graphic Illustrations
>
> - Should have all necessary components to assure comprehension.
> - Should be stand-alone in nature.
>
> Highlights
>
> - Should have clear, concise, correct, and complete writing.
> - Should be statements of fact only.
> - Judgmental statements should not be included.
> - Should be stand-alone in nature.
> - Should have no more than three included for any graphic illustration.

Displaying the Data: Some Examples

Example 1:
This first sample comes from the NCA materials and focuses on State Assessment Data and contains an appropriate balance of graphical and written explanative information.

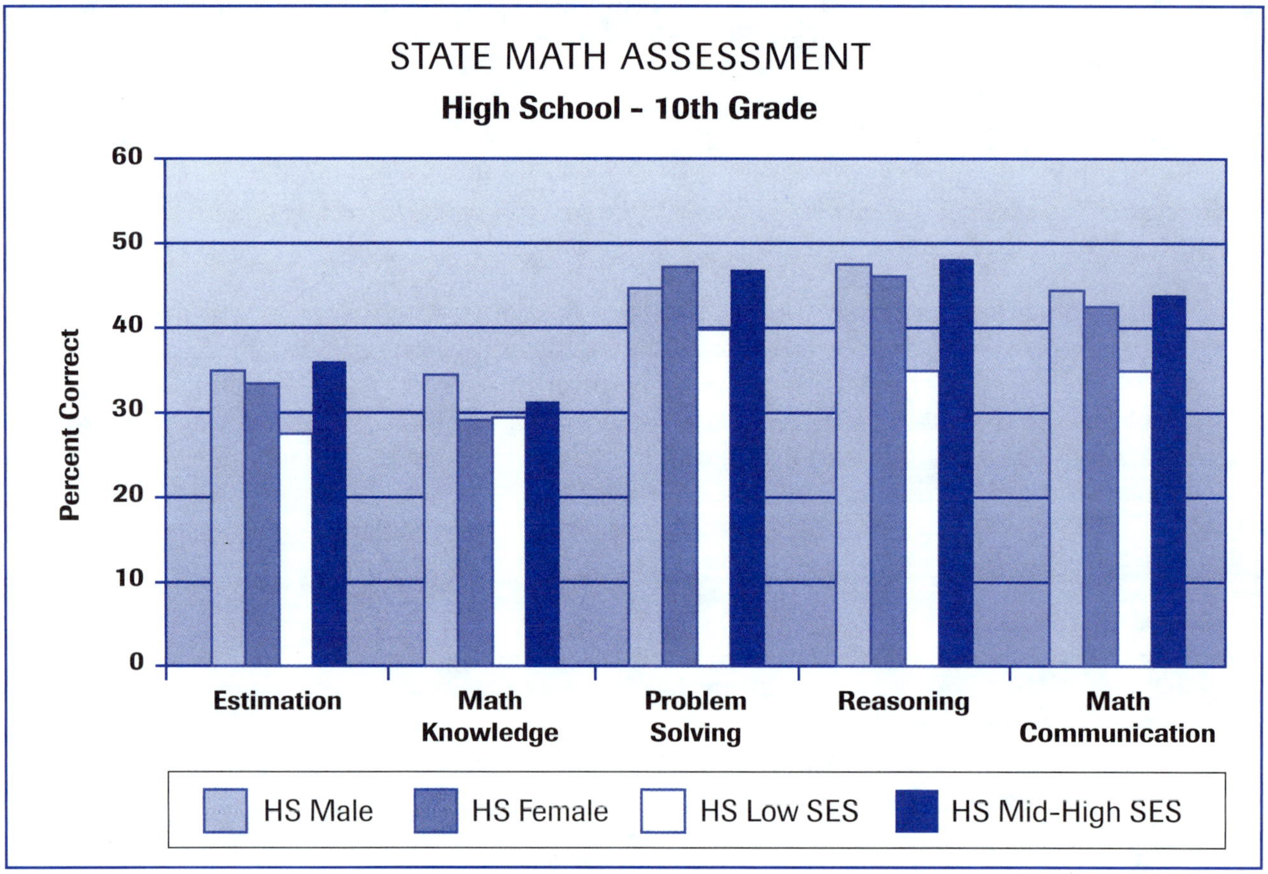

The state testing examination information is in five areas of mathematics (estimation, math knowledge, problem solving, reasoning, and math communication). The scores are reported in two disaggregations: gender and socioeconomic status.

The state average scores are compared to our scores below:

State Averages		High School Averages
37.8	Estimation	32.95
38.2	Math Knowledge	31.08
50.7	Problem Solving	44.27
53.3	Reasoning	43.86
50.1	Math Communication	41.08

The school scores are below the state average scores in all five categories.

Example 2:
This second example is again provided by the NCA.

Graduate Survey Results

Two hundred eighty-three graduates responded to a survey one year after they graduated. The following chart illustrates the opinions of respondents who are currently enrolled in some post-high school education as: 1-excellent, 2-good, 3-average, 4-below average, 5-poor.

The graph represents the percentage of the 283 respondents who selected each rating for the five categories: overall preparation, math, English, science, and computer skills.

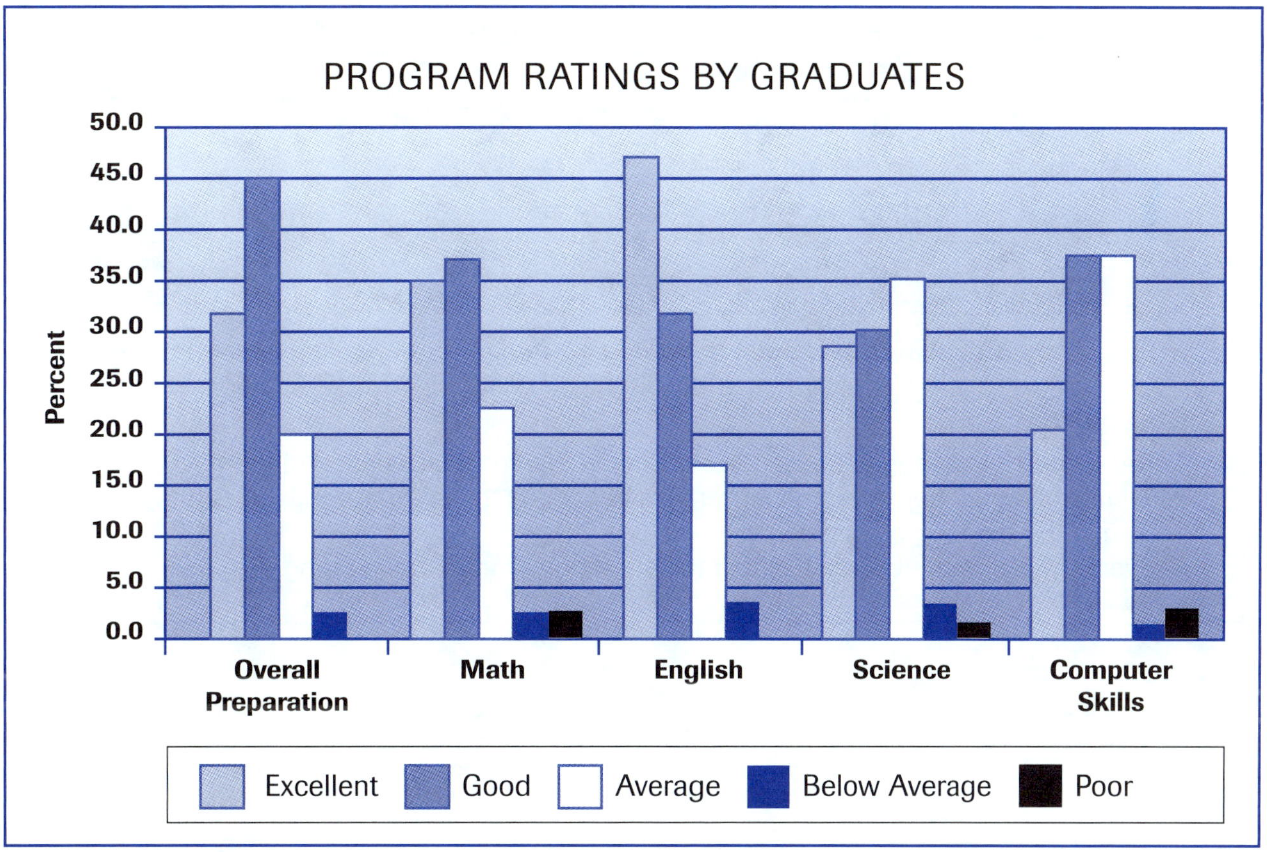

Key Findings: Seventy-seven percent of the students replied that their overall preparation was excellent or good. No student replied that the overall preparation was poor.

Keeping in mind that the first group to examine the profile is the faculty, this graph would be a good piece of information to share and celebrate.

These third and fourth examples are provided by Edie Holcomb in her 1999 book *Getting Excited About Data. How to Combine People, Passion, and Proof.*

Example 3
Absences by Class Period

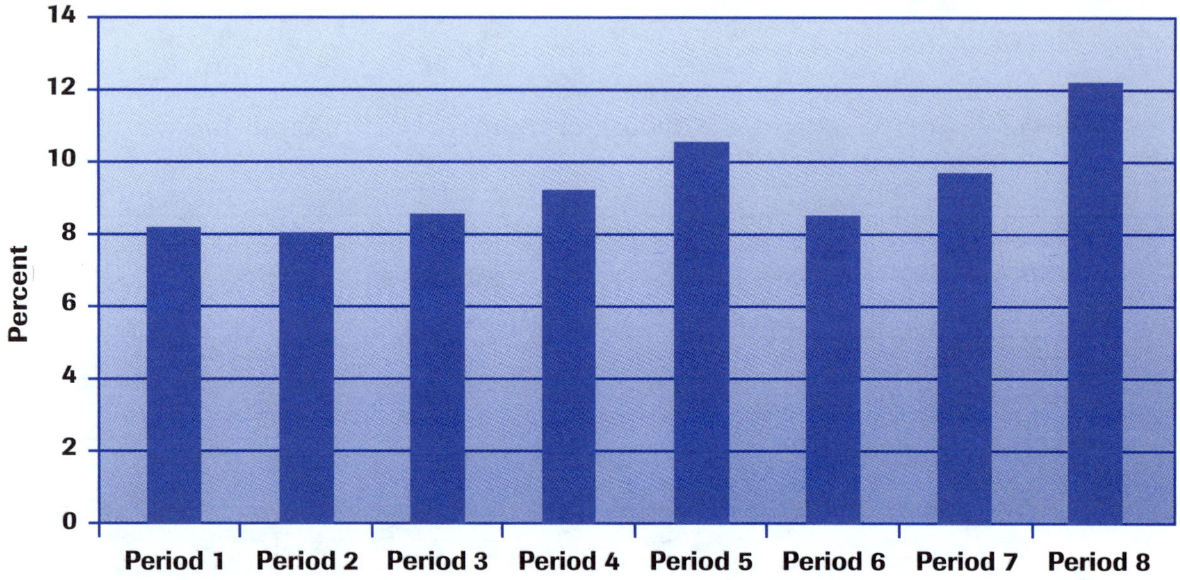

Observations:

1. The highest percentage of absentees occurs in the final class period of the day.
2. There is a higher percentage of absentees in periods that are part of the lunch cycle than in the morning class periods.
3. Overall, more students are absent in the afternoon than in the morning.

(Holcomb, 1999)

Example 4
Scores on Standardized Test of Elementary Math Disaggregated by Socioeconomic Status (SES)

All students in grades 2-5 take the standardized test every October. These are the results for this year's students in each grade level. Qualification for free or reduced price lunches is used to identify students as having lower socioeconomic status (SES). The percentile rank indicates that our students scored higher than such a percentage of students taking the test nationwide.

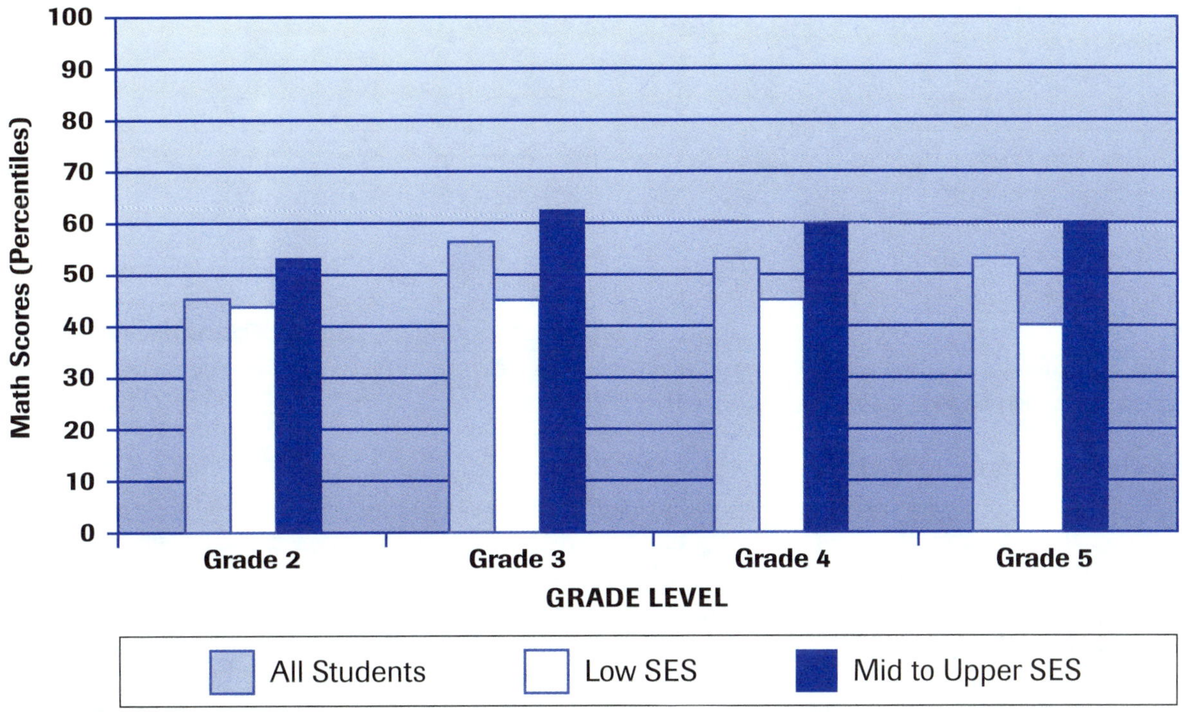

Strengths:

1. The means of math scores for all students in grades 3, 4, and 5 are above the 50th percentile.
2. The mean math scores for middle and upper SES students are above the 50th percentile at all grade levels.

Concerns:

1. The mean for all 2nd grade students is below the 50th percentile.
2. At all grade levels, lower SES students score below middle and upper SES students. The discrepancy ranges from 7 percentiles on the second grade test to 20 percentiles on the 5th grade test.
3. It appears from this data that lower SES students fall further behind in math as they progress through the grades.

(Holcomb, 1999)

Holcomb (1999) argues that the selection of material for a School Profile is a two-stage process: choosing the data that will be considered meaningful, relevant, and useful to a school's staff, students, and constituents and then deciding how to display the data so it is clear, accurate, and user friendly. A first consideration, she says, is size. She stresses the need to be selective about how much of all the available data to compile in a document that will be reviewed and discussed by all stakeholder groups. Holcomb explains:

> **Many principals I work with have at least one 4-inch three-ring binder of data about their school and students. It's available to anyone who wants to review it. They also have the mini-version: a small 1/2-inch binder or packet of data that is used for discussion purposes. Guidelines from the North Central Association of Colleges and Schools recommend a collection of about 20 pages, with only one or two data displays per page.**

A second consideration, she says, is how to display the data. Her contention is that there are three major parts of a data display: the introduction or explanation, the graph (or other kind of tabular display), and the summary statements or findings.

The **Introduction** should take the form of a short paragraph which explains what test was used, who and how many were tested, when the test was given, and how it was analyzed. Such a paragraph should define the terms used—such as *socioeconomic status* (SES)—and differentiate terms such as the *percentage* (say, 30%) of students who scored at a particular *percentile* (say, the 70th).

The **Graph** should include clear labels on each axis. It is important to give a clear sense of the range of scores used, particularly on the vertical axis. If the data is in percentiles, the full range from 0 to 100 should be shown. If the school's scores are all below the 70th percentile, for example, the graph should not be cut off at the 70th just to save space as this might mislead the readers into thinking that the achievement level is higher than is actually the case.

The **Summary** should contain factual observations, not evaluative judgments and should aim to provide indications of both strengths and concerns/challenges.

With the advice provided by Edie Holcomb and the NCA very much in mind, Holly and Lange (2002) listed these quality criteria for a School Profile.

1. Is it <u>complete</u>? Does it have all the sections of the recommended format?
2. Is it <u>representative</u>? Does it contain input from all stakeholder groups?
3. Is it <u>comprehensive</u>? Does it cover all the major areas of school life?
4. Is it <u>adequate</u>? Does it contain enough relevant information from which to identify some priority issues worthy of attention?
5. Is it <u>informative</u>? Is the data well displayed and accompanied by useful, brief commentaries ('captions')?

6. Is it communicative? Is the profile understandable to laypeople and user-friendly? Could it be understood by, and an appropriate learning vehicle for, the members of various constituencies/stakeholder groups?

7. Is it action-able? Does the profile provide enough material to inform goal-setting and action planning?

8. Is it current? Is the information in the profile kept up-to-date and maintained over time to show longitudinal trends and change patterns?

The Contents of a School Profile

The last question to tackle is what to include in a School Profile. One quick response is that the information in the profile has to be both broad and specific. It has to be broad enough to support both the initial identification of needs and goals and, as it is maintained and added to over time, the demarcation of new needs and goals. It has to be specific enough to be able to target the identified goals and track their progress in data over time. This bi-level use of school profile data is well evidenced in Sioux City, Iowa. Each building is encouraged to amend its five-year Comprehensive School Improvement Plan on an annual basis by studying both levels of data: cumulative and goal-specific.

As previously mentioned, NCA schools are given specific advice in terms of what to include in a School Profile. According to NCA guidelines, although the school profile for each school is considered unique, the outline has to follow a uniform structure, as follows:

School Profile Outline

Cover Page
Table of Contents
School Mission Statement
Data

- Unique Local Insights
  (Display of information collected from questionnaires, surveys, opinionaires, interviews from people who know the school best.)
- Follow-Up of Former Students
  (Graduates, dropouts. Reports from students, receiving teachers [e.g., middle schools, high school, and universities], as well as employers.)
- Existing School Data
  (Information already in the school data-base related to students, instruction, community.)

Dubuque Community School District in Iowa took the basic NCA structure and amplified it for use with all elementary, middle, and high schools in the district. The format used is divided into two sections, as follow:

Section I: Executive Summary

This is an introduction and is written by the school principal in narrative form (3–5 pages). Its purpose is to

- provide an opportunity to describe the unique characteristics of the school;
- offer a summary of the achievements, gains, and progress made, and the new, emerging priorities;
- list the support programs and interventions being implemented.

It is grounded in the data from the three parts of Section II: School Profile, shown below, and is collated by the Superintendent and used to report to the School Board on an annual basis.

Section II: School Profile

This has three parts:

A. Progress Review on the Comprehensive School Improvement Plan

B. School Data-Base (incorporating the NCA frame)

C. School Improvement Process Summary

Bernhardt Meets NCA

As in the previous chapters of this workbook, it is possible to produce a planning framework for constructing a Profile at the School Level by combining Bernhardt's four kinds of data with the NCA frame for producing a School Profile, as follows.

SCHOOL PROFILE PLANNING FRAMEWORK	Student Learning	Demographics	Perceptions	Processes
Unique Local Insights	1	2	3	4
Follow-up of Former Students	5	6	7	8
Existing School/ Student Data	9	10	11	12
Instructional Data	13	14	15	16
Community Data	17	18	19	20

This planning matrix consists of 20 cells, each of which can be activated by using a trigger question.

Cell 1: What are the perceptions of the various groups in the total school community (faculty, staff, administrators, students, parents, business partners, and community members) concerning the current performance levels of student learning?

Cell 2: How do these perceptions vary across various demographic groups?

Cell 3: What are the unique characteristics of the local school community?

Cell 4: What are the strengths and challenges of the local schooling process as seen from the perspectives of those who know the school best?

Cell 5: According to former students, what was their degree of preparedness for the next level of their education?

Cell 6: How do the responses to 5, 7, and 8 break down in terms of demographic groups?

Cell 7: According to former students, what were the strengths and deficiencies in their academic preparation?

Cell 8: According to former students, which programs, classes, and instructional strategies worked best for them?

Cell 9: What are the data saying about achievement levels and student learning results over time?

Cell 10: How do these data look when broken down for various demographic groups?

Cell 11: How do the various demographic groups perceive their levels of academic performance?

Cell 12: Which processes (programs, classes, grade levels, and strategies) currently work best in terms of student achievement?

Cell 13: In what ways are the teachers using student assessment data to adjust their instruction?

Cell 14: In terms of differentiated instruction, how are the students' different learning styles being taken into account?

Cell 15: What are the stakeholder perceptions of the new instructional strategies being used in the classroom?

Cell 16: What programs and strategies are being introduced to meet the changing learning needs of students?

Cell 17: How are community resources being used to support student learning?

Cell 18: What are the demographic changes occurring in the community and how is the school adjusting to these changes?

Cell 19: How do the participants perceive the level of community support for the school?

Cell 20: What processes and strategies are being used to strengthen the links between the school and the community?

These 20 key questions can be used for various purposes such as the following:

- Organizers for the School Profile
- Pointers to "holes" in the available data
- Issues to be explored in data analysis
- The basis for participant reflection
- Criteria for success

Tracking Implementation Efforts

In terms of using data to monitor implementation efforts over time, Holly and Lange (2002) composed this planner—again, based on the Bernhardt model.

IMPLEMENTATION PLANNER

Kinds of Data	What has to be tracked? -Elements	What data will be needed?	How?	When?	At what level? -District -School -Classroom	Who will track and record?
Student Learning/ Achievement						
Demographics						
Client/Customer Satisfaction/ Perceptions						
School Programs/ Implementation Strategies						

(Holly and Lange, 2002)

A Data Profile at the School Level
Task 8: The "Ideal" School Profile

Purpose: To plan the contents of the "ideal" school portfolio/school profile.

Grouping: Work with your Learning Team.

Directions: This is a major task for your team. Based on all the advice given in this chapter, decide what are the essential elements to be included in a school profile/school portfolio. Discuss which elements are most essential and why.

Essential Features of a School Profile

A Data Profile at the School Level
Task 9: Promoting EFFECTS at the School Level

Purpose: To provide review questions to be asked of the school level.

Grouping: Work on your own and then meet with your Learning Team.

Directions: On your own, review this chapter and reflect on the following question: In what ways can a school level data profile promote each aspect of the EFFECTS model? Using the chart on the following page, be as specific as possible as you link a school level data profile with the EFFECTS model. Meet with your Learning Team to share completed charts.

EFFECTS	Specific ways a school data profile promotes EFFECTS
Establishing clear expectations.	
Feedback being provided to the learners in progress reviews.	
Formatively screening for the purpose of diagnostic intervention.	
Examining, reflecting, and making decisions on the strength of the data.	
Committing to personal goals and growth plans.	
Taking responsibility for implementing and monitoring the plans.	
Summatively assessing progress toward desired learner outcomes.	

CHAPTER 5

CHAPTER FIVE: USING A DATA PROFILE AT THE DISTRICT/LOCAL SYSTEM LEVEL

As at other levels of the local educational system—the classroom/teacher level and the school level—the first responsibility is to support the previous level. The teacher's task is to support the learning of each and every student, the school's task is to support the learning and development of each and every teacher and classroom, and, in turn, the district's task is to support each and every school. Indeed, as Richard Elmore (2002) argues:

> Insofar as districts are going to be part of this [reform] enterprise, they are going to have to prove that they can provide capacity to schools to enhance learning....It's not just a matter of releasing people to do what they already know how to do. It's making available the skill and knowledge for people to do things that they have not yet been able to do or not yet learned how to do—and that involves connecting people to sources of knowledge and skill outside of their own workplace; connecting people within the workplace to develop knowledge and skill; and substantially increasing professional development that is instructionally focused and designed to enhance student learning. "Capacity" also means putting teachers and principals in a stream of professional knowledge that lies outside of their immediate workplace and encouraging them to bring it into the workplace.

The Evolving Role of the District

Elmore (2002) argues that schools should base their decisions on external research and benchmarks. In so doing they should look outside for practices likely to work in their settings and should commit to more focused work on professional development. The task of districts, he says, is to make all these things happen. Elmore also maintains that the school is the primary unit of accountability and—according to the principle of reciprocity of accountability and capacity—the district has the obligation to provide the kind of support necessary to sustain accountability for change efforts over time. His argument would suggest, therefore, that while the school is the primary unit of accountability, the district is the primary unit of support.

In the post-*NCLB* period, however, districts and, indeed, states are also major units of accountability. Moreover, while the support function is an important one, there is much more to what a district can do (and be) than just performing this one particular—albeit important—role. There are five reasons for making this point.

1. As an extension of Elmore's argument, the district is the "broker" in the process of matching the schools' internally-identified needs with externally-generated, scientifically-researched implementation strategies. Slavin (2003), Cawelti (2003) and Doyle (2002) have all recently made this same point. Moreover, Carnahan and Fitzpatrick (2003), Killion (2003) and Feuer, Towne, and Shavelson (2002) have all argued that the way to avoid being buried in an avalanche of research is for educators to becoming more discerning, more savvy consumers of external research. In Slavin's case, he welcomes this new trend in education:

> **[Previously] In education reform…research has played a relatively minor role. Untested innovations appear, are widely embraced, and then disappear as their unrealistic claims fail to materialize. We then replace them with equally untested innovations diametrically opposed in philosophy, in endless swings of the reform pendulum….At long last, education reform may be entering an era of well-researched programs and practices.**

Reliable and valid evidence, emphasizes Slavin, should be the force that drives change. One of the district's responsibilities, therefore, is to be the discerning conduit that filters these well-researched programs and practices in terms of their "fit"—both with the locally identified needs and the nature of the local context. The questions to ask of these research-based strategies are: "Do they work?" and "Do they work in places—and with students—like ours?"

Killion (2003) recommends that districts base their professional development activities on a "What Works" approach and Denis Doyle (2002) reminds us that data-driven decision making and scientifically-based research are related concepts that contribute to "knowledge-based decision making."

> **Evidence and the data that comprise them are to be preferred to flying by the seat of your pants. And as knowledge is power, data are its raw material. The systematic use of data lies at the heart of scientific method, which is why the two ideas connect (Doyle, 2002).**

Scientifically-based research, says Doyle, tells you *what* to do and data-driven decision making, at the local level, relates to the *how* to use it. As Doyle concludes:

> In a scientific era, what could be more estimable than making decisions based on careful research and compelling evidence? **Research holds the promise of helping us understand what works.**

The district, therefore, is continually replenishing local change efforts by applying intelligence about what works in similar settings elsewhere and this information is then translated into implementation by means of local data-driven decision making.

2. The district is the local educational **system**. As such, systemic problems can be identified and responded to systemically. Indeed, many of these problems only emerge into the light of day when identified on a system-wide basis. According to Dennie Palmer Wolf (2002):

> **Across the country, administrators in many districts are face-to-face with stubborn problems in the area of adolescent literacy. Far too many high school students can't read or write at more than the note or shopping-list level. Many of these same districts are stunned to realize that their 17- and 18-year olds got this far without such fundamental skills and habits of mind. Yet rarely do districts or schools think about the long-term history of students' literacy learning. Still more rarely does a faculty have the chance to reflect on where these patterns of adolescent literacy may be rooted. But schools can take steps to change this....It can (and perhaps should) begin at the most local level.**

Case Example

Wolf (2002) cites the following example of one district's efforts to approach a systemic problem systemically. Working with protocols developed at the Annenberg Institute for School Reform, the principals and literacy coordinator of a medium-sized district decided to take their colleagues' inquiry beyond examining test scores. As a consequence, they committed to the following steps:

1. They called on teachers in all subjects, K–12, to collect assignments in which students engaged in informational reading and writing (stories, reports, essays, and so on) throughout one particular month.

2. Teachers were also asked to collect the completed assignments from a sample of currently *successful*, *competent* (average), and *struggling* students.

3. Using a professional development day, teachers spread out their samples from the *competent* students, making a developmental progression from K to 12 across the gymnasium floor.

4. Working in inter-disciplinary teams, teachers examined the work developmentally, noting where they observed new, rising expectations, plateaus of unchanging expectations, and "cliffs"—sharp rises in expectations.

5. Using these data, teachers sketched the growth trajectory that they saw implied in the assignments and the resulting student work.

6. In a debriefing session, the participants shared their observations and identified major trouble spots where student growth was clearly foundering.

A Data Profile at the District/Local System Level Task 1: Applying a Systemic Approach

Purpose: To use the case example for team planning.

Grouping: Work with your Learning Team.

Directions: Working as a team, design a similar K–12 "event" for your district. Use the following outline to guide your work.

Subject area(s):

Grade level(s):

Inquiry/focus area(s):

Type(s) of assignments to be collected:

Sample range of collected assignments:

Process for reviewing:

Process for recording findings:

Process for sharing findings/debriefing:

3. Unlike in England where each school has its own elected Board of Governors, in the U.S.A., of course, it is at the district level that local governance occurs. As Robert Klempen (2003) has recently reminded us, the district level is the school board level and this decision-making body also needs to be data-driven. Moreover, one of the functions of a school board is to represent the local system and, in rising above sectional and vested interests, to make sound, impartial decisions that cannot be made at the sub-system level.

   Klempen (2003) cites the case of the school board in La Crosse, Wisconsin, which needed to develop a new enrollment plan for the district's students. Mismanagement of this issue, says Klempen, could have polarized the community, driven a wedge between the school board and administration, alienated faculty and compromised educational quality. As a consequence, Superintendent Thomas Downs insisted on using a clear, systematic, and agreed upon thinking process for making tough decisions. It was vital to have a "clean" process and, therefore, to use a thinking process that would allow a step-by-step approach to organizing the information and making the judgments needed to arrive at a sound conclusion. According to Klempen, "situation appraisal," "problem analysis," "decision analysis," and "potential opportunity analysis" are four examples of such a process.

   In the case of La Crosse, those involved decided to use a combination of situation appraisal and decision analysis, thus enabling them to "cut through all the clutter," keep everyone focused on the search for information and solutions, and tap into the best thinking of stakeholders and the larger community to achieve the desired results. They also agreed to use a facilitator to ensure objectivity and to safeguard the decision-making processes.

Situation Appraisal

The purpose of this three-stepped process is to achieve clarity by talking through, struggling with, and identifying and agreeing upon the main issues involved.

Step One is the brainstorming stage during which participants are asked to identify all the important issues. In the La Crosse case, this step produced a "gold-mine" of some 50 issues.

Step Two involves whittling down the issues into a more manageable number of the most relevant ones—30 in La Crosse.

Step Three invites participants to cluster the issues and to agree upon "umbrella" concept definitions for each cluster.

Decision Analysis

This involves the following steps:

- Developing a decision statement.
- Setting objectives.
- Clarifying the objectives.
- Weighing the objectives.
- Generating and comparing alternatives.
- Assessing risks.
- Making the best-balanced choice.

A Data Profile at the District/Local System Level Task 2: Improving the Quality of Decision Making

Purpose: To discuss how such approaches could be applied to improve district-level decision making in the participants' school systems.

LT

Grouping: Work with your Learning Team.

Directions: In your team, discuss how these approaches might be applied locally to improve the quality of decision making in terms of both process and product.

4. In representing the entire local community, the district not only has to rise above sectional interests and stand for the common good, but also has to compensate for "faults" in the system. Three such examples are all a result of what could be called the downside of the *No Child Left Behind* legislation.

   - According to Wolf (2002), in an article entitled "When Raising Isn't Rising," many accountability systems, like *NCLB* itself, fail to measure student growth over time. She argues that, in its insistence on the cross-sectional analysis of, say, 8th grade data annually (as opposed to tracking longitudinal, cohort data from grade to grade), *NCLB* uses an attainment, as compared to a development, model of accountability. Consequently, she concludes:

     > **Any move to developmental models for accountability will have to take root at the local level. It will be forward-looking school administrators, teachers, and community leaders who will play the major roles in beginning a conversation about achievement that focuses on continuous growth.**

   - According to Linn, Baker, and Betebenner (2002), the reliance on cut scores in terms of standardized test results (to identify the numbers of students who are "proficient" for *NCLB*) represents a limited approach to attainment and further militates against student growth and development.

     > **Attending only to a single cut score, whether it is at the proficient or basic level, gives schools, districts, and states credit for increases in performance only when students make it past the cut score. This narrow focus does not give schools credit for increases in student achievement that occur in the broad range—either below or above the cut score. Schools where the vast majority of students score far below the cut score in a given year might make great improvements in student learning that shows up in only a small fraction of the students scoring above the cut score the following year. Substantial increases in the percentage of students who are near the cut score (or who are performing better than their peers the previous year but are still below the cut score) go unrecognized if only increases in the percentage above the cut score are credited (Linn, Baker, and Betebenner, 2002).**

   Again, it will be up to district administrators to correct this imbalance and recognize credit-worthy student achievement that occurs beyond the confines of *NCLB* attainment levels.

- Henry Mintzberg (1994), in a seminal article entitled "The Fall and Rise of Strategic Planning," argues for a balance between not only formalized planning (characterized by "analysis") and the more creative, but less formalized "synthesis" of ideas, but also the use of hard and soft data for planning purposes.

> **The problem with the hard data that are supposed to inform the senior manager is they can have a decidedly soft underbelly. Such data take time to harden, which often makes them late. They tend to lack richness; for example, they often exclude the qualitative. And they tend to be overly aggregated, missing important nuances....The big picture is painted with little strokes (Mintzberg, 1994).**

Again, it is the responsibility of district-level personnel to reap the benefits of both aggregation and the nuances that come with disaggregation, the big picture and the little strokes, the quantitative and the qualitative.

5. It should be noted, therefore, that aggregation and disaggregation are both important. Indeed, in terms of data analysis, disaggregation is only made possible by aggregation. Parts, by definition, are a function of the whole. Moreover, aggregated data speak to general trends, while disaggregated data allow for "slicing and dicing." Stephanie Hirsh (2003) reminds us that using disaggregated data entails carefully examining data to ensure that educators understand the impact of any measure on various sub-groups of students. It is the district's responsibility, therefore, to create a **data system** that honors the importance of both aggregated and disaggregated data.

A Data Profile at the District/Local System Level
Task 3: Benefits of Aggregating and Disaggregating Data

Purpose: To reflect on the benefits of both aggregating and disaggregating data.

LT

Grouping: Work with your Learning Team.

Directions: Working as a team, list the benefits that accrue by both aggregating and disaggregating data and discuss the target groups of the various benefits.

Benefits of Data Aggregation

Benefits of Data Disaggregation

The System Level

It is at this fourth system level—the district—that the most energy is currently being generated, partly as a response to the requirements of *No Child Left Behind*. It has to be said, however, that many local school systems, like those mentioned in the introduction to this workbook, were already making the kind of moves described below.

Historically, say Noyce, Perda, and Traver (2000), many school districts underutilized one of the most powerful and common symbol systems available to them—numbers—to monitor, evaluate, and revise programs and policies. This, they say, has been rapidly changing. According to these same authors:

> **Imagine instead that district decision makers pay close attention to numerical patterns to help determine how well schools are doing and what they should do next. As a result, schools recognize gender disparity, commit themselves to gender parity, and develop action plans to remedy the problem. In addition, decision makers request that the building-level administrators and teachers continue monitoring the representation and success of boys and girls in mathematics and science courses, charting the results periodically to measure policy effectiveness. They use a similar approach to determine and adjust the district professional development plan. When districts and schools use data to make decisions, they have the makings of a data-driven school culture.**

In order to become this kind of district, the will (to do things differently) and the capacity both have to change. The will to be different in terms of the use of data is changing and this partly stems from the ownership and commitment currently being generated at the district level. And, while each district is a disaggregate of state-level data, it is also an aggregate of all the data generated at the local level. It is districts that have to report to state departments and their communities, although, under the auspices of *NCLB*, individual schools are being asked to share the limelight. The district is and will remain, however, the "parent," umbrella organization.

A Data Profile at the District/Local System Level Task 4: Local Accountability Efforts

Purpose: To provide evidence of the local accountability measures being taken in the participants' school systems.

LT

Grouping: Work with your Learning Team.

Directions: Working as a team, list the ways that your local school district is currently moving to meet its accountability obligations.

Local district accountability efforts:

Changing Capacity

In addition, as mentioned in the previous chapter, the will to use data is changing because the capacity is changing. Computer systems are revolutionizing the collection, storage, retrieval, and use of data. What these systems do is ease the flow-through of data across the system levels—thus aggregation and disaggregation are triggered with the push of a button—and the same data can be used for various purposes at different system levels. Moreover, the district is the system when it comes to computerized applications.

Noyce, Perda, and Traver (2000) cite the example of a district with a population of 23,000 students (15% of whom are eligible for free or reduced lunch) that recently invested in the creation of a student information management system. According to the same authors:

> The information system currently helps the district address two important issues. It provides quick and tailored responses to building and staff requests for student information, and it enables teachers to design classroom instruction that accounts for the needs of individual students on the basis of their reading, writing, and numerical proficiencies. For example, the district can monitor transience more efficiently and meet the needs of students who move among district schools within the year.
>
> The cornerstone of the system is a student-specific, numerical ID. The ID tracks students through the school system. Each record contains student and parental background, coded as variables, as well as information about attendance, scheduling, grades, and disciplinary action. The new system all but replaces the cumbersome paper-based filing system previously maintained by the district.
>
> At the classroom level, teachers have direct access to individual student data through student performance software....The software provides teachers with a **comprehensive, quantitative profile** of each student based on cumulative grade-by-grade records.

According to one of the participating teachers:

> Teachers can research areas of difficulty for various students. At weekly meetings, these teachers can target class-wide areas of weakness and adjust their classroom instruction to address these problems. At the same time, teachers can address individual problem areas with those students through one-on-one instruction.

The student data enables the classroom teachers to undertake "diagnostic teaching" and introduce targeted interventions to improve the learning of both individual and groups of learners. Meanwhile, data from the same information system can be used to convince those at the school level to amend their attendance policy and those at the district level to change the professional development plan so that it is better aligned with student and, therefore, instructional needs. The following diagram represents this multi-leveled use of data.

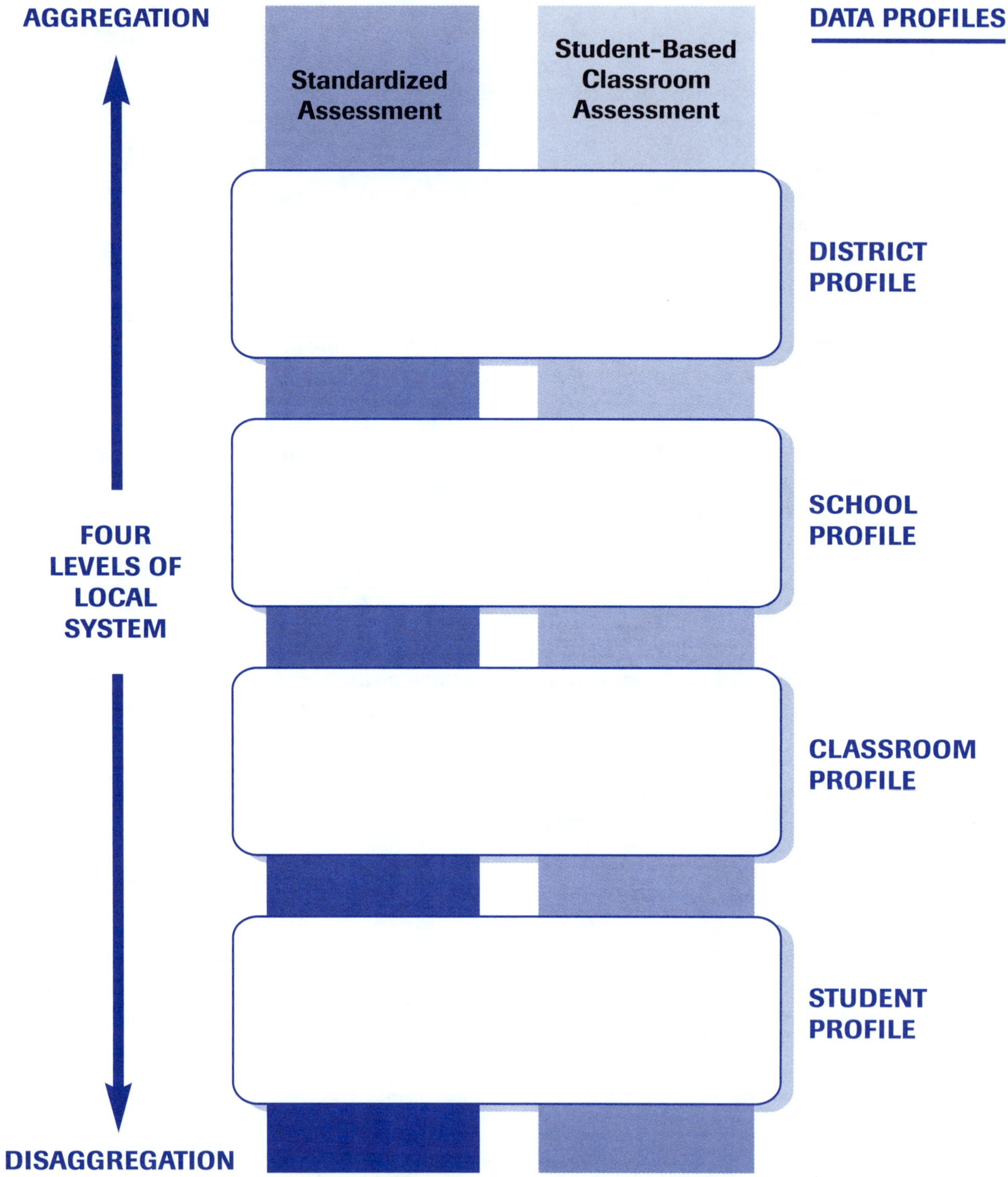
AGGREGATION
Standardized Assessment
Student-Based Classroom Assessment
DATA PROFILES
DISTRICT PROFILE
SCHOOL PROFILE
FOUR LEVELS OF LOCAL SYSTEM
CLASSROOM PROFILE
STUDENT PROFILE
DISAGGREGATION

Data-Based Decision Making at the District Level

Over the last two years or so, journals and periodicals for educational administrators have included countless articles concerning data-based decision making at the district level. For example, in the American Association of School Administrators' (AASA's) April 2001 edition of *The School Administrator*, entitled *Data-Driven Decisions* and subtitled *New Ways to Get Answers: the "Drill-down" and the "Walk-through,"* several school districts report on their efforts to become data-driven systems.

Theodore Creighton (2001) sets the tone for this particular publication by arguing that statistical strategies, not gut feelings, form the hallmark of good instructional decisions. In fact, he says, data-based decision making has replaced "shooting from the hip" as the way to make forward progress. As a consequence, data need to be gathered and examined in a systematic way using statistical analyses. The problem with educators using statistical approaches on an everyday basis is that, generally speaking, statistics instruction for teachers and administrators has lacked four important components.

First, such instruction tends to lack relevance (most college level classes, he contends, are taught as a hard-core mathematics course devoid of powerful and practical applications relevant to school administrators and student learning); second, it does not fully integrate current technology (such as GB STAT, SPSS [Statistical Package for the Social Sciences], and Microsoft Excel); third, it is not designed for educators and the problems they face on a daily basis; and fourth, it treats statistical analysis as a tool to be used in conducting research projects and dissertations, not to help summarize, organize, and simplify data (in terms of percentile ranks, means, median, modes, range, and standard deviation).

Creighton argues:

> **Statistics is not advanced mathematics. The majority of statistical analyses useful to administrators can be completed with a basic understanding of mathematics and is more conceptual than requiring complex calculations. Statistics is a set of tools designed to help describe the sample or population from which the data were gathered and to explain the possible relationship between variables.**
>
> **A superintendent might wonder if the mathematics instruction in his district's schools is being delivered in a manner that treats boys and girls equally....A simple statistical procedure called the Pearson correlation can help identify a relationship between math scores and gender (a simple stroke of the computer keys with the help of EXCEL, GB STATS or SPSS). If the results of the analysis point to a pattern of boys receiving higher scores in mathematics on standardized tests, the principal may want to**

> look more closely at classroom instruction to determine if perhaps instructional strategies can be altered to address the equity issue.

Creighton concludes:

> Collecting data without purpose is meaningless. All too often, school leaders fail to formulate decisions based on data. The effective use of data must play a major role in the development of school improvement plans. It helps us identify students who are improving and those who are not and helps to identify the reasons.
>
> Meaningful information can be gained only from a proper analysis of data rather than intuition and gut feelings. The administrator can serve as instructional leader as data-driven decision-making and instructional leadership go hand in hand.

In the same publication, Raymond Yeagley (2001) describes one district's use of the Quality School Portfolio (QSP) software, developed by the Center for Research in Evaluation, Standards and Student Testing (CRESST) at UCLA. The Quality School Portfolio is an easy-to-use database and one of several tools currently available for integrating and analyzing school data. As Yeagley explains, it has the capability of loading records from any source that exports to a text file. Moreover, according to Yeagley:

> **Analysis tools in QSP permit multiple levels of disaggregation,** provide automatic tracking of goal progress based on the indicators matched to those goals, support cross-sectional and longitudinal analysis and include reporting functions with graphs, tables and "dashboard" displays that make the information clear and easy to understand.

In describing the work with the Quality School Portfolio in Rochester N.H., Yeagley says that four principles were applied:

1. Data were used to identify district, school, and classroom strengths and weaknesses.
2. Staff training was deemed essential for the effective use of data (including the use of some basic statistical approaches).
3. Communicating the results in a clear, concise, accurate manner was always seen as a vital component.

4. Inviting feedback from constituents, it was recognized, closes the loop.

It was also understood from the outset that asking good questions is a priority activity. As Yeagley explains:

> **A more productive approach is to start with probing questions that will get at the heart of the district's performance, then find the data and new ways to assess the data that will answer those questions.**

The Quality School Portfolio, says Yeagley, encourages broader inquiry by integrating (and aggregating) information from a number of sources to identify previously hidden patterns in student learning and other aspects of school operations. For example, the district can now look at the common characteristics of students having difficulty with a specific skill or set of skills and be able to ascertain whether the problem lies in the same feeder school, among the same demographic group, or in the fact that a particular reading series is used in the lower grades.

Yeagley suggests that a seven-step process be used to ease the use of data.

- Use a unique student identification number that follows the student from kindergarten through graduation.
- Plan your database and, before importing any information, create a data map that identifies the name, source, and target of each data element. This provides consistency to facilitate longitudinal analysis, accommodate student transfers, and simplify the importation of data.
- Think of new ways to look at old data.
- Don't reinvent the wheel. Excellent resources are available to help in designing a data system from the ground up, such as those developed by the National Forum on Education Statistics.
- Involve everyone. According to Yeagley:

> **Create a central data team that includes the superintendent, a board member, principal, curriculum coordinator, and teacher. Our buildings also have data teams that include principals, guidance counselors, teachers, parents, paraprofessionals, and others. We anticipate adding others, including students in the upper grades.**

- Take data to the school and classroom levels. It makes eminent good sense to involve those at the school and classroom levels in the collection of data, so, by investing in the process, they are much more likely to implement the changes that are identified as being necessary.

- Choose a data integration program that fits your needs and resources. As Yeagley concludes:

> **Some districts may need an extensive data warehouse like that used in Tucson; others may be ready for a sophisticated statistical package such as the Statistical Package for the Social Sciences, or SPSS. Most will be best able to work with an off-the-shelf product like QSP, Socrates, or eScholar. Regardless of size, budget, or needs of the district, the right tools are available.**

Philip Streifer (2001), in the same AASA magazine, describes the "drill-down" process. This starts with a global question or issue (e.g., Is there a major under-performing group of students in this district and why?), which then is broken down into its component parts for analysis. This process involves drilling down through layers of data to identify the root issues.

Drill-downs are very much part of what another AASA article calls the new "lingo" of data-driven decision making (itself more often than not shortened to DDDM). Drill-downs are similar to "data mining" and "data digs." Working from a large data-base (or "data warehouse"), the aim is to do the following:

- Use disaggregation of data to get more and more specific about a problem and its root causes.

- Explore the correlations between various factors.

- Achieve a much deeper understanding of the issues involved.

- Use data analysis to such a fine degree (using statistical procedures if necessary) that our current assumptions are challenged and tested.

Drill-downs show us that, while the fourth level of the local system—the district—is the aggregation of the student, teacher, and school levels, it is possible to probe vertically down through the layers to find answers to our questions. Electronic information management systems have created this capability and, in so doing, have rendered the membranes between system levels extremely permeable.

Moreover, Philip Streifer, the author of the article on drill downs, was formerly the Superintendent of Avon Public Schools in the 1990s (he is now an Associate Professor of

Educational Leadership at the University of Connecticut) and it is interesting to note his comments about his district work:

> I took a systems approach. I looked at various operations of the district, how they planned, conducted program evaluations, the kind of data they looked at. I asked questions about the degree to which each program was supported by good organizational structures, what links existed to professional development.

Based on his experience at both district and university levels, Streifer has concluded that data-driven decision making is the inescapable future of educational administration. One-fifth of the coursework in the Educational Leadership Program at the University of Connecticut is devoted to the subject. Streifer states:

> That's a huge departure from when I was trained, but times have changed. People realize education can't be pushed forward any more based just on hunches. You've got to have good information thoroughly analyzed.

These comments, while amplified in Streifer's 2002 AASA book *Using Data to Make Better Educational Decisions* (co-authored with Richard Kisiel), are contained in an article entitled *Data-Driven Districts* (Lafee, 2002) which, along with several other linked articles, can be found on the AASA's *School Administrator* Web Edition.

Scott Lafee describes the work of four districts, nationwide, that have taken different tracks to using data to inform key decisions. In creating the backdrop for their work, Lafee points out that, while some districts were already changing and adjusting to the new demands for data-driven decision making, *No Child Left Behind* has certainly accelerated their efforts.

> The call for greater accountability means administrators and teachers must show proof—tangible, statistically valid evidence—that what they are doing is working, that students are learning faster and better.
>
> The old tools of education—intuition, teaching philosophy, personal experience—do not seem to be enough anymore. Virtually every state has put into place an assessment system intended to measure and validate student achievement and school performance.
>
> The passage of *No Child Left Behind* only raises the stakes further, adding new responsibilities for states, districts, and

> schools to accurately and promptly collect, analyze, and report data on student demographics and achievement. Federal law now requires annual state reports on student performance by gender, race, disability, income, migrant status, and English fluency. States also must report how many students were not tested, in the same categories, and provide detailed information about the professional qualifications of those teaching the students, such as the percentage of classes taught by teachers lacking certification in their subjects.

Educators, says Lafee, feel compelled to show they're getting good results. The onus for accountability and reporting is mainly on states and districts. It is the district that is the local unit for planning and reporting purposes. Because many districts are fast becoming data-using systems, however, the student, teacher, and school levels will also become part of the drive for local accountability.

In the Lafee article, Geannie Wells, former director of AASA's Center for Accountability Solutions, points out that these moves toward data-based decision making at the local level are not always plain sailing. While lots of data are generated, they are not always used well. Moreover, she says:

> Ownership of data has been a problem. Some data reside at the state level, the district level, the school level, or even with vendors in proprietary formulas. Incompatibility of various data systems has been a problem. Often enrollment data can't be tracked with student achievement data or program participation data, etc. Inadequate funding and technical support for data collection have been challenging. And data from testing companies and states are often not disaggregated to such a level that they can be useful and are not available in a timely fashion.

These are all issues that educators everywhere will recognize. One major problem with the technology of data-based decision making seems to be that the conceptual understanding of what can be done often outstrips the capacity to do so. Moreover, everybody isn't starting at the same place. People don't have the same tools (technology and technicians to handle it). As Lafee (2002) comments:

> Only 16 states, for example, have systems that give each student a unique identification number that allows them to be tracked and assessed over their entire school career. Only 17 states provide demographic breakdowns of student achievement by race or family income on school report cards.

In terms of the work of the four school districts described in the Lafee article (Plainfield, NJ; Palo Alto, CA; Francis Howell in St Charles, MO; and Rio Rancho, NM), various common themes emerge.

1. The need for a standards-based accountability and information system that looks both ways: internally and externally. According to Joshua Starr, Plainfield's director of accountability:

   > You have to have a system that external entities like the state or the public could use and understand, but also one that is embraced by those who have to work within it. We wanted a system that engendered the best aspects of internal accountability, that promoted critical inquiry based on accurate data by all stakeholders, that had regular checkpoints but in a nonthreatening environment for decision makers.

2. The first step is simply gathering together all the available data, i.e., data warehousing. According to Starr:

   > Basically, what you're trying to do is build a giant repository of knowledge, a database that is accessible to everyone in the district who can make use of it to benefit students. The challenge with schools is that data typically reside in so many places, all of them different. It takes a huge commitment of time, funding, and energy at every level to build an effective data warehouse. Some large districts have done so, but not many....So I contracted with eScholar (one of numerous educational software companies with data management programs) to help us gather and organize data—student information, attendance figures.

3. The next step after gathering the data in one place and in an "electronified" (Starr's word) state is to begin to explore the potential benefits of disaggregation and cross-data analysis. For example, Starr says he can take simple data like attendance and test scores and combine them in different ways, broadening or narrowing the point of interest. In Palo Alto, says a local spokesperson, the data were mostly aggregated "in monolithic collections of information that were hard to break apart or use when seeking particular answers." In recent years, however, the district has pushed hard to disaggregate the information, breaking it down by gender, socioeconomics, ethnicity, and other categories.

4. The disaggregation of data at the classroom and individual student levels allows for diagnostic teaching and the mounting of targeted interventions. In Palo Alto,

an intervention program called "Kid by Kid" has been implemented which is clearly data-driven and data-intensive. It draws upon a host of informational sources: state-mandated tests, content standards tests, writing tests, and various diagnostic tests that are given at the beginning of a school year to establish baseline abilities. One of the goals of this program is to be able to monitor each child's development throughout the year and, armed with this information, be able to effectively intervene in each child's learning. In Rio Rancho, working within the Baldrige framework for organizational assessment and development, staff members conduct weekly classroom evaluations of students in order to review progress, pinpoint learning issues, and mount targeted interventions.

5. In Rio Rancho, as in the other districts, it is very much "a work in progress." As such, it is recognized that professional development for all those involved is a key component. Beginning with central office staff, a training program was taken to all buildings so that all administrators and faculty members could work on pertinent program components. Professional development is seen as a key to the continued success of the system.

The AASA's Mission

Clearly, the American Association of School Administrators (AASA) has invested in the growth of data-based decision making in schools and school districts. Evidence of this commitment includes articles in the monthly magazine, *The School Administrator*; the publication of Streifer and Kisiel's 2002 book, *Using Data to Make Better Educational Decisions*; the establishment of the Center for Accountability Solutions; and the excellent, informative Web Edition of *The School Administrator*. Currently, Web-based articles that are available include:

- "Data-Driven Districts"
- "Providing Data to Your Board"
- "The Will and the Way of Data Use"
- "The Lingo of Data-Driven Decisions"
- "A Forum for Becoming Data Savvy"

In addition, there is an excellent section listing additional resources.

In the article entitled "A Forum for Becoming Data Savvy," Raymond Yeagley (2002) recommends the work of the National Forum on Education Statistics. According to Yeagley:

> **I've discovered the forum is a terrific vehicle for preventing me from reinventing many wheels or from having to revamp my**

> district's data-collection processes to meet federal standards. With enactment of *No Child Left Behind*, the need for local school leaders to understand data collection and use has moved squarely from the "nice to know" into the "absolutely crucial" area.
>
> The forum, in conjunction with the National Center for Education Statistics, has a wealth of free, high-quality reports that can inform the work we do as school district leaders, especially as we try to meet new state and federal reporting mandates.

In another article (entitled *Providing Data to Your Board*), Linda Dawson (2002) argues:

> The times are changing, and the savvy superintendent now realizes that good data, presented in the context of board-adopted and district-wide goals for student achievement, can move a board to focus on core performance issues. Those include supporting administrative means to improve achievement while advocating for moral and fiscal support of district efforts throughout the community.

This should be done, she says, by abiding by four guiding principles:

- Insist that the Board establish district-wide goals or end results for student achievement.
- Assist the Board in receiving targeted, customized training on what data are and are not to measure whether student outcomes are being achieved.
- Insist that the Board adopt a code-of-conduct policy on data use.
- Provide the data on time, with an executive summary and in an understandable presentation.

AASA is not the only organization that is strongly advocating for the use of data-based decision making. In the magazine, *District Administration* (October 2002), in an article entitled "Data Digs," Melissa Ezarik says that everybody's talking about data—getting it, using it, and sharing it—and data-driven decision making can be just what a district needs to help at-risk students. As with the articles mentioned above, Ezarik talks to district people who are trying to activate data-based decision making in their local systems.

One district, for instance, is using the Quality School Portfolio to gain skills in using disaggregated data. According to Ezarik, this approach is likely to especially benefit those students who are at risk of not succeeding in school. First, they will be identified and, second, the combination of factors that contribute to their "at-riskness" will become all the more apparent, thus paving the way for intelligent interventions to be mounted.

As Anthony Dallmann-Jones, director of the National At-Risk Education Network, comments, if administrators start to gather data with the intent of developing a needs-based curriculum, "...you see reparation start to happen down the line in schools" (Ezarik, 2002). Dallmann-Jones, in touching on one of the themes of this workbook, also argues that every student considered at-risk should also have **a student profile with a needs assessment** that examines academic, social, psychological, health, emotional, and behavioral needs, so instruction can be tailored and targeted.

In another district, teachers have instant Web access to classroom data through their Educator's Assessment Data Management System (EADMS)[2], which disaggregates data on the ESL population and other subgroups. This system allows teachers to obtain student profiles and make curricular and intervention decisions accordingly. Collecting student data that link to district goals is key.

Other data-gathering tips suggested by Ezarik include:

- Develop a district plan for a data-driven culture.
- Do an audit of data types, location, format, and value in decision making.
- Start with a broad question, "What do we need to know?"
- Involve teachers.
- Recognize that tracking at-risk students now requires action later.

Ezarik also adds some words of advice for using data for needs discovery, intervention, or program development relative to at-risk students:

- One number doesn't tell all.
- Consider ranking students on a 1 to 5 at-risk scale.
- Look for patterns by disaggregating data.
- Don't get lost in the data.

Another organization that is encouraging the use of data-driven decision making is the National Association for Elementary Principals (NAESP). Its recent book entitled *Essentials for Principals: Data-Based Decision-Making* (2001) raises awareness of the need for the same student learning and achievement data to be used for decision making at every level of the local system.

---

[2] Educator's Assessment Data Management System (EADMS) is a data management system designed by Adrylan Communications.

> Education leaders are beginning to see the power of using this same [standardized test] assessment data, along with data gathered from carefully designed classroom-based assessments, **to improve instruction at the school, classroom, and student level** (NAESP, 2001).

According to this publication, as many educators are already aware, a major task is to build classroom-based criterion-referenced assessments that pass the tests of technical adequacy and can be used consistently and reliably over time for the recording, reporting, and reinforcing of student learning. A major consideration is that the "goal posts" (the content standards and benchmarks) are not moved because only then can the kind of consistency and reliability that is required be built into the assessment system. This is a major undertaking that is currently under way in countless schools and school districts across the nation. And these content standards are system standards and apply equally to all local subsystems.

As with the AASA's Web Edition of *The School Administrator, Education Week* has its own Web site that contains *Data Driven: An Occasional Series*. In the June 12, 2002 edition, Lynn Olson tells the story of a superintendent who was asked by a parent why his 11th grade son was being scheduled for Spanish when he still couldn't read English competently. Shouldn't he be enrolled in a reading class instead? The query sent the superintendent off in search of data: how many students in grades 7–12, he wondered, were reading below the 4th grade level? Within fifteen minutes, the Ohio superintendent had his answer and he found that 84 students fell into that category. Based on this information, the district was able to design a more targeted reading program for those students and, within the first year, the district was seeing grade-level growth, on average, in excess of a year and a half. If he had gone through the 3,000 paper files, said the Superintendent, it would have taken him weeks and weeks; instead, thanks to a Web-based data analysis and decision-support system known as SchoolNet,[3] he was able to drill down and get those names in 15 minutes.

According to Olson:

> Such experiences are making...school leaders believers in the power of analyzing data to improve public education. Although the practice goes by a variety of names—business intelligence, data warehousing, decision-support systems, data-based or evidence-based decision making—the idea is the same. By knitting together the thousands of data elements now collected by districts and states into a centralized computer bank, educators can look for patterns that could help improve both the management and productivity of schools.

[3] http://www.schoolnet.com

Clearly, electronic information management systems like SchoolNet and eScholar[4] are power tools for school districts to use in becoming more data-driven. Olson points out, however, that a similar transformation is taking place at the state level, where states ranging from Georgia to Michigan to Mississippi are creating huge warehousing systems to link everything from student test scores and enrollment figures to teacher information and financial data. Meanwhile, she says, Michigan and Pennsylvania have contracted with Standard and Poor's School Evaluation Services[5] to provide the public with Web-based access to information about the performance of individual districts and schools. Olson lists a number of other state initiatives as follow:

- Georgia lawmakers mandated the creation of a comprehensive educational information system in 2000 as part of the A-Plus Education Reform Act.
- In 2001 the Denver-based Education Commission of the States joined with the University of Texas at Austin and Just for the Kids, an Austin-based nonprofit organization, to form the National Center for Educational Accountability. The center's goal is to improve states' knowledge of how to use data to monitor, analyze, and improve student and school performance. The center currently has data for six states—Arkansas, Florida, Minnesota, Tennessee, Texas, and Washington—that together represent 19% of the student population of the United States.
- The Council of Chief State School Officers, the National School Boards Association, and the American Association of School Administrators also have launched projects to work with districts on the collection, analysis, and use of data.

Ultimately, says Olson, the hope is that the push to data-based decision making will also help teachers and principals. She cites the case of Broward County in Florida—one of the first and largest districts to enter the data warehousing field—where in 2002 every teacher received a detailed analysis of how each of his/her students performed on every subtest of the state assessment system. If a student performed below the passing grade in an individual area, such as fractions or statistics, the report flagged it. According to Phyllis Chasser, the senior data-warehouse analyst for the Florida district:

> **The whole idea is that all this information is there, but if we don't get it out to teachers, who can then change the way they teach,...it's useless to have the information.**

According to the same Ohio superintendent who was able to follow up the parent's literacy question:

> **I think what it does, with the ease of use, is allow us to move away from voodoo education, where we're just shooting in the dark**

[4] http://www.escholar.com

[5] http://ses.standardandpoors.com

about what the issues are with students, and to become much more professional in our delivery of instruction, assessment of instruction, and description of interventions for kids.

A Data Profile at the District/Local System Level
Task 5: Assessing Local Strengths and Challenges

Purpose: To reflect on the extended commentary on data-based decision making.

Grouping: Work on your own and then meet with your Learning Team. Select a group recorder.

Group process strategy: Use a consensus-building strategy when meeting with your Learning Team. Have a group recorder create team lists.

Directions: Having read the extended commentary on data-based decision making in school districts across the nation, provide a list of the strengths (the areas in which your district is keeping abreast of these developments) and the challenges that your district is facing. Share your lists with your Learning Team and develop team lists of district strengths and challenges. Use the space below for note taking.

Strengths

Challenges

Data Warehousing

In her latest article entitled *No Schools Left Behind*, Victoria Bernhardt (2003) returns to her thesis that schools and districts need to collect four kinds of data and then, for the purposes of data analysis, use them in intersection with one another. Bernhardt gives the example of a school where 60% of third graders scored below the proficient level on the state's criterion-referenced reading test. Consequently, the staff disaggregated the below-proficient third grade scores (student learning data) by looking specifically at gender and ethnicity (demographic data) and asking the question: "Were there differences in the way a particular ethnic group was taught?" (process data) and, on the student questionnaire results: "What did they think were their teachers' attitudes to the likelihood of them succeeding in school?" (perception data).

This is the kind of drill-down process, says Bernhardt, that can be facilitated through the creation of a system database or data warehouse. Indeed, conceptually, data warehousing does not have to be confined to only very large districts. A district—whatever its size—can gain from the installation of a database/data warehouse. In establishing such a facility, says Bernhardt, districts should build in six features:

1. Accessibility at different levels

   Here Bernhardt is validating the basic concept that underpins this workbook: that data stored at the district—and possibly even the regional and state levels—should be accessible to educators to inform their decision making in their schools and classrooms.

2. Automatic graph builders

   Any analytic tool should be capable of producing easy-to-understand charts, tables, and graphs.

3. Disaggregation on the fly

   Users should be able to gain access to the next deeper levels of data analysis quickly and easily.

4. Intuitive point-and-click or drop-and-drag technology

   Users should be able to apply these techniques without having to refer to a manual.

5. The ability to follow individual and group student achievement across grade levels, pre-K through 12

6. Fast and easy creation of standard reports

Concerning the use of a data warehouse, Bernhardt (2003) has two pieces of good advice to offer. First, the district should hire an expert data analyst to perform the major analyses required for the district and each of its schools, thus releasing teachers to spend their time studying the results of the analyses instead of having to produce the analyses themselves. Second, teachers deserve data support in some basic ways. Bernhardt explains:

> **They should be able to start the school year with historical data on each of their students and a full picture of what students already know and what they need to learn. And they should use ongoing measurements to make sure that all students are progressing and mastering the content.**

In these and other ways, a well-constructed and well-administered data warehouse can service the necessary reflection and decision making that has to occur at each level of the local educational system.

Lawrence Rudner and Carol Boston, in their article "Data Warehousing: Beyond Disaggregation" (2003), argue that educators should use the onset of *No Child Left Behind* as the opportunity to retool and systematize their data collection, reporting, and analysis. In this same article, Rudner and Boston quote Kimball and Ross as follows:

> **Properly constructed, a data collection and analysis system can go beyond simple disaggregation to provide information more fully responsive to local, state, and federal data needs. Such a system allows many school personnel, not just in-house statisticians and programmers, to generate reports and analyses that supply information, provide accountability, explore relationships among different kinds of data, and inform decision making. A data warehouse is a system specifically structured for such query and analysis (Kimball and Ross, 2002).**

Once such a system is in place and the data is collected, Rudner and Boston argue, it can be used for multiple—both traditional and new—purposes.

Traditional Purposes

- Monitoring compliance with federal and state law and standards
- Responding to federal reporting requirements
- Determining state-funding allocation
- Tracking school performance

- Assigning sanctions and rewards
- Responding to data requests from state legislatures and local boards of education
- Producing annual statewide summary publications
- Designing school improvement plans

New Purposes of Data Warehouses

- Transforming mountains of data into useful information and helping policymakers identify and plan responses to key trends

  Like businesses that use information to maximize their competitive stance, say Rudner and Boston, educators can use a system with high-quality data to improve and maximize learning.

- Presenting the entire local picture of education (including school facilities, staff, students, attendance data, achievement data, and program data), thus allowing the study of its functioning over time

  Such analyses can help identify trends, predict events, and guide anticipatory action. Questions that can be answered include:

  - Does the district have a pending teacher, administrator, or paraprofessional shortage?
  - What are the likely demographic changes in the student body?
  - Can the district expect a declining enrollment?

  Data warehouses can help examine trends in retirement rates, new hires, certification types, teacher age, and student numbers to aid in short- and long-term planning.

- Supporting two types of data—cross-sectional and longitudinal—to create what Rudner and Boston call "a more complex and nuanced picture of school performance" than just reporting test scores from year to year.

Cross-Sectional Data

Cross-sectional data consist of all those different kinds of data that intersect with and impact growth in student achievement. For example, say the same authors, just reporting reading achievement annually means that other pertinent data sets and their effects are ignored. Corresponding variations could have occurred in county enrollment and class size; the percentage of students receiving free and reduced-price meals might have risen; the percentage of students in special education or ELL classes might have increased; the number of new teachers might be greater than usual.

All these factors could have impinged on the students' test scores. Indeed, the statistical techniques of regression analysis allow us to assess the relationship between the dependent variable—the test scores—and the combined effect of several independent variables. Thus multiple correlations with demographic factors allow us to paint a more complex picture of local trends than just rising or falling test scores alone. It is cross-sectional data that help us move beyond simple disaggregation by allowing us to make more detailed breakdowns and trace the interplay of factors that determine the success (or not) of various demographic groups.

Longitudinal Data

Data warehouses permit analyses of groups (cohorts) of students as they progress through the grades. Consequently, more meaningful data about educational gains is produced than comparing, say, fourth grade scores year by year.

A Data Profile at the District/Local System Level
Task 6: Data Warehousing

Purpose: To respond to the need for data warehousing.

LT

Grouping: Work with your Learning Team.

Directions: As a team, decide what your district has to do to create a data warehouse. What is already in place? Prioritize your next steps. Use the space provided on the following page for planning.

Data Warehousing—Next Steps

The District Data Profile

Many of the features of the School Data Profile can be the same at the district level. Indeed, the District Profile is mainly an aggregate of all the School Profiles. It can be constructed using the same Bernhardt-NCA matrix and the same 20 key questions. As the district is the main unit of reporting to the state and local community, however, the District Profile needs to be constructed with the various reporting requirements very much in mind.

Each district, in order to meet the stipulations of *No Child Left Behind*, will need to gather, store, retrieve, and report on an annual basis the following data:

- Student performance data in three core content areas (reading, math, and science) at grade levels 3–8 and another high school grade (probably grade 11)

  These performance data will need to be disaggregated by gender, race, disability, income, migrant status, and English fluency.

- The numbers of students not tested in each of the above categories
- Attendance, dropout, and graduation rates disaggregated by the same demographic categories
- The professional qualifications of teachers and the percentage of classes taught by teachers lacking certification in their subject areas

A Data Profile at the District/Local System Level
Task 7: Meeting the Requirements of *No Child Left Behind*

Purpose: To use a checklist to review local district progress toward meeting the demands of *No Child Left Behind*.

LT

Grouping: Work with your Learning Team.

Directions: Use the following checklist (currently being used by the author with school districts in Iowa) to review your district's progress toward meeting the stipulations of *No Child Left Behind* by deciding:

1. What is already in place?
2. What needs work?
3. If work is needed, when will it be done?
4. Who will be responsible for carrying out the work?

DISTRICT CHECKLIST FOR *NO CHILD LEFT BEHIND*	In Place	Needs Work	When	Who
Content Standards and Benchmarks				
Reading, Math, and Science				
Grade Level Expectations				
Grades 3–8, 11				
Assessments				
For students at grade levels, content areas, and years of *NCLB*				
Aligned with content standards				
Adequate technical quality				
Multiple measures (with at least one norm-referenced)				
3 achievement levels (with "proficiency" as combination of top two levels)				
Sufficient # of students assessed				
Adequate Yearly Progress				
Goals for all grade levels tested, all content areas, all (sub-) groups				
Disaggregated by SES, race, disability, gender, and ELL				
Graduation rate				
Attendance				
NAEP testing—4th and 8th reading and math				
Teachers' qualifications (% teaching their subject)				
Annual Report Card				
Comprehensive School Improvement Plan				

The District as the Local School System

The district is the local system and, as such, returning to the analogy of the Russian dolls, it is the largest of the identical dolls within which the others are folded. In what amounts to a nested arrangement, the system level incorporates the other three levels. Thus, in a very real sense, the district is only as good as each student, each classroom/ teacher, and each school that constitute the local system. As it is a system, however, systemic properties come into play that result in the district being more than just the sum of its parts. A district has a "value-addedness" that only a system can possess. This is particularly true when it comes to the district being a data-using system.

The District as a Data-Using System

While districts may not have lived up to their potential as systems in the past, this is rapidly changing, especially in terms of their data-use.

- Each district can be a repository (a warehouse, if you will) of data from various sources, both internal and external. These data can be collated, stored, processed, and, at the appropriate times, made into reports for the other three local system levels. This means that each school would get its own comprehensive but summary data report, to be added to its School Profile, to be used in its annual planning process. The same would be true for each classroom teacher and each individual student.
- The district as a data-using system benefits from the power of data aggregation. It is at the district level that, in terms of the overall collection of data, the "big picture" emerges, locally speaking. It is within aggregate data that patterns emerge: indeed, it can be argued, the more data that are available, the more patterns become distinguishable. As statisticians have always told us, the more members of a given population that constitute the "sample," the smaller the margin of error. Moreover, it is the aggregation of data that makes disaggregation possible. A part of something, by definition, is only a part when there is a whole to relate to. Disaggregating data ("slicing and dicing," one colleague calls it) involves looking at one subset of the aggregate data and studying the performance of that subset relative to the performance of the whole or against success criteria that are expected of the whole and, therefore, each of its parts.
- The Law of Reciprocal Data Use means that data can flow up and down the local system and be used for aggregation and disaggregation (remembering that each level above is an aggregation of the level below and each level below is a disaggregation of the level above). This means that the power of both aggregation and disaggregation can be harnessed several times over within the same local system. If the power of aggregation lies in its holism, the power of disaggregation lies in its specificity. Disaggregation helps us become much more diagnostic, focused, and targeted in both our interventions and our resource allocation. It's a case of sharpening the optics.

- The same data (such as standardized test scores) can be used to inform practice at each level of the local system. Consequently, individual students, individual classroom teachers, individual schools, and the individual district can all study their slice of the data and ask the same question, "What does this mean for me (or us)?" Having answered this question, those at each level can take appropriate, relevant remedial action. Data-driven diagnostic interventions can occur on a regular basis during cycles of continuous improvement at each of the interlocking system levels. This is the EFFECTS model at work in a multi-layered local setting.

- Given the powerful potential of electronic information management systems, it is increasingly possible to argue that the more centralized and uniform the system used, the more decentralized can be the decision making that flows from it. It's another variation on the aggregation/disaggregation theme. It's also a question of consistency of inputs, whether they are content standards, assessments, grades, grade level expectations, or so forth. If the fact that all students, teachers, and schools are being held to the same learning expectations is the dependent variable, then how they get there becomes the independent variable. As Richard Stiggins (1997) has said, if you hold the learning expectations still long enough and carefully explain to the students what they are, then the students are so much more likely to achieve them (but maybe not at the same pace). This same principle applies at the other system levels. From a technical standpoint, what is crucial here is the compatibility of computer systems and software packages so that, electronically-speaking, the local system becomes seamless and all participants can add to and take from the accumulating database.

- There is one fallacy of the ownership argument. Of course, ownership is a powerful factor in how people feel about membership in and changes of their organizations. That's incontrovertible. But, as teachers like to remind us, why spend precious time reinventing the wheel when a perfectly good wheel already exists. This is why, as part of their involvement and exploration at their particular level and in the right learning climate, educators would not be adverse to data reports being prepared for them at the district level.

  Increasingly, teachers are turning to the author and making such comments as, "Why am I collecting this data when I know they already have it in the district office?" We can work much smarter when it comes to data collection, data storage, and data retrieval and who does what in the overall process. Those at each local level receive from the level above, apply this information at their level, and pass on the relevant parts to the level below, while at the same time, passing information upwards through the system. This is what makes teachers, administrators, and staff members, particularly at the classroom and school levels, such pivotal figures. They contribute data and receive data reports that are partly based on their contributions. They appreciate this level of support. In addition, this aspect of giving and receiving mirrors the Janus role for teachers that is mentioned throughout this workbook. As Keefe and Jenkins (2002) have observed, the teacher is

> ...the instructional specialist closest to the learning situation who best understands the needs and interests of students as well as the policies of the school and of the district.
>
> In the kind of learning organization envisioned in this workbook (one that is characterized by the principle of reciprocity), those at each level 'give so they shall receive.'

A Data Profile at the District/Local System Level
Task 8: Promoting EFFECTS at the District Level

Purpose: To provide review questions to be asked of the district/system level.

Grouping: Work on your own and then meet with your Learning Team.

Directions: On your own, review this chapter and reflect on the following question: In what ways can a district data profile promote each aspect of the EFFECTS model? Using the following chart, be as specific as possible as you link a district data profile with the EFFECTS model. Meet with your Learning Team to share completed charts.

EFFECTS	Specific ways a district data profile promotes EFFECTS
Establishing clear expectations.	
Feedback being provided to the learners in progress reviews.	
Formatively screening for the purpose of diagnostic intervention.	
Examining, reflecting, and making decisions on the strength of the data.	
Committing to personal goals and growth plans.	
Taking responsibility for implementing and monitoring the plans.	
Summatively assessing progress toward desired learner outcomes.	

CHAPTER 6

CHAPTER SIX: REFLECTIONS

Five Cautions and Five Commendations

Reflecting on the contents of this workbook in the light of what other commentators have to say, the author offers five cautions and five commendations.

Caution One: School Improvement Plans should release change initiatives, not stifle them.

Schmoker (2003b) has recently cautioned us on relying too heavily on over-elaborate, over-blown, over-complicated school improvement plans that serve to distract us from our real task—the hard work of improving teaching. There is no substitute, he says, for teams of teachers meeting regularly—and continuously—to design, test, and then adjust their lessons and strategies in the light of their results. Yet, he continues:

> The typical school or district improvement plan takes us in an entirely different direction. I've received hundreds of these "strategic" or "comprehensive reform" plans from around the country. Almost none of them make these simple collaborative structures the soul of their improvement planning; most don't include them at all.
>
> More typically, strategic plans contain a dizzying, incoherent abundance of activities and responsibilities within columns and categories reading: 'Goals'; 'Action Plan' (or 'Action Steps'); 'Objectives'; 'Timeline'; 'Resources Needed'; 'Evaluation'; 'Target Areas'; and more. Superficially, they are large, handsome documents; school boards, district offices, and accreditation agencies love them.

While these plans have what Schmoker calls "graphic elegance" and are put together with the best of intentions, they represent a "bankrupt model," the first casualty of which is clarity. Schmoker continues:

> The best schools and organizations know that no one can pursue more than about 2 goals at once and expect results. The plans I see set an average of half a dozen or more. These, in turn, unleash—and become confused with—a torrent of promises to implement an exhaustive array of popular but unproven programs, initiatives, and name-brand teaching fads....[Yet]

> some schools are succeeding mightily with simple plans that focus on the collaborative structures essential to improving instruction.

Many of the current plans are more political than practical, he says; in some elaborate form of bureaucratic window-dressing, they give the impression that much is being done. Schmoker concludes:

> It is time to close the gap between what we know and what we do to promote learning. It is still the rare school that recognizes that teachers, working together, have the capacity—right now—to improve instruction. We need to give them this opportunity. We need to ditch much of what we now do, in exchange for regular times, at least monthly, for teachers to design, refine, and assess their instructional strategies. And then, just as regularly, we need to honor and celebrate each team's success as its members develop and share better lessons and strategies with their colleagues. It is no overstatement to say that in most schools, such practices would yield immense, often immediate, benefits. All of this is within our reach. School districts, state departments of education, universities, and accreditation agencies, all with their considerable clout, could lead the way. Our school teachers and students deserve no less.

Caution Two: Beware of the inadequacies of systemic reform.

One of the commentators cited in Schmoker's article, Michael Fullan (1996), has explored much the same terrain and concluded that "systemic reform" is not all that it's cracked up to be. Like Schmoker, his claim is that many of our attempts to undertake systemic reform merely add to, rather than solve, the ongoing problems of change overload and fragmentation. As Fullan (1996) maintains:

> This situation would seem to be an ideal candidate for "systemic reform" which promises to align the different parts of the system, focus on the right things, and marshal and coordinate resources in agreed upon directions. The idea of systemic reform is to define clear and inspiring learning goals for all students, to gear instruction to focus on these new directions, and to back up these changes with appropriate governance and accountability procedures....There is [however] a fundamental flaw in the reasoning that leads us to conclude that we can resolve the problem by attending to systemic alignment.

Systemic alignment, he admits, does work in the "top half" of the system. At this level, creating alignment, clarity, and consistency of policy will definitely help. What is also required—in the "bottom half" of the system—is greater coherence and clarity "on the receiving end, not the delivery end." Fullan continues, "What looks like clarity at the top may increase clutter at the bottom."

Indeed, in the search for greater, shared, subjective clarity at the doing end of education, Fullan (1996) sees two strategies—networking and reculturing (the process of developing new values, norms, and beliefs concerning instruction, assessment, and new forms of professionalism)—as having the greatest potential. These strategies, he says:

> **...help to develop and mobilize the conceptions, skills, and motivation in the minds and hearts of scores of educators....You cannot improve student learning for all or most students without improving teacher learning for all or most teachers.**

Caution Three: Don't rely solely on the formalized, pre-programmed approaches normally associated with strategic planning.

Schmoker's article makes reference to the work of James Kouzes and Barry Posner and their assertion that strategic planning doesn't work because it detaches strategy from operations, thinking from doing. Henry Mintzberg (1994), in his paper entitled *The Fall and Rise of Strategic Planning*, was the first to make this claim. Mintzberg, however, doesn't write off strategic planning completely. After all, the title of his article does include both the fall *and rise* of strategic planning. His argument is that there should be room for both strategic programming (what he refers to as the calculated, analytical, formalized, deliberate, and rational approach to planning) and strategic thinking (which he describes as the creative, informal, intuitive, non-linear approaches associated with the learning process). It's a case, he says, of accommodating the analytical thinking of right-handed planners *and* the creative thinking of left-handed planners.

Caution Four: Don't undermine the power of people to act as agents of change.

Peter Block (2001 and 2003) touches on many of the issues raised above. One of the problems with expert-led, compliance-driven models of change, says Block (2003), is that they serve to de-skill and de-motivate the very people who have to make the changes happen. Spirit, will, and courage (the vital ingredients of a change mentality), he says, all wither in high control, punitive situations. We become stymied and reticent to act.

> **Individually and collectively, we have the wisdom we need to get the results we want. The challenge is to trust and act on the wisdom. How many times have we brought in an outsider to tell us what we already knew was true....My presumption is that we have all the skills, the tools, the training that we need (Block, 2003).**

Yet, he continues:

> Seeking certainty in human affairs breeds doubt and the belief that we are not enough....Seeking certainty assumes that if we knew more or knew better, we could know what to do. We think there is a right way, that someone else knows what it is, and that it is our job to figure it out. And the world conspires with this illusion, for it wants to sell us an answer.

Are we being efficient, he asks, about the things that really matter? Moreover, he responds:

> Greater efficiency, getting tough on evaluation and control doesn't change one child's life.

When it comes to change, therefore, Block (2003) gives this advice:

- Don't try to coerce change. Indeed, he says, people resist coercion much more strenuously than they resist change (see also Duffy [2003] on this same subject).
- Invite consent. In an inclusive and invitational environment, people are put in charge of their own futures.
- Stop being a victim. People see themselves as an effect rather than a cause. This has to be reversed, he says, so that we decide what the world is to become and we declare that we are responsible. We have to realize that we cause our effects and we have to stop blaming others for our problems.
- Do what matters. People, he says, always find the time to do the things that really matter to them.
- Stop giving opinions and calling them *the truth*.

Caution Five: Don't rely solely on data-based decision making.

Echoing Peter Block, Denis Doyle (2002) reminds us of the importance of professional judgment. Data-driven decision making contributes to professional judgment, he says, but is not a substitute for it. Block goes on to say:

> The mantra data-driven decision making is so powerful and appealing that to some it may seem to be a substitute for informed judgment. This it should not do. Indeed, there is no substitute for professional norms or the hard won knowledge of the experienced

> teacher or administrator. Data-driven decision making does not replace professional judgment. It is the handmaiden of professional judgment. It informs, it elaborates, it improves, but it is not a substitute for it....Knowledge-based decision making [is] a blend of scientific evidence based on data and hard-won professional judgment that, taken together, is that mix of intuition, insight, and experience that we think of as wisdom.

It's a case, he says, of blending artistry and science.

These five cautions offer much food for thought. In responding to them, the author presents five commendations.

Commendation One: All the approaches included in this workbook should be applied with simultaneity and flexibility.

The four levels of the local educational system—the student, the teacher/classroom, the school, and the district—should not be seen as another version of a bureaucratic hierarchy.

- The four levels should be interactive, reciprocal, and, therefore, catalytic. What is being sought is the power of synthesis.
- The four levels should be operated with a democratic intent. In fact, the more that the local data-using, multi-leveled system becomes "electrified," the more potential it has for democratizing education at the local level. Computerized data-use has the potential of involving local educators across system boundaries, in real time, and in dialogues that challenge the subjective world of classrooms with the objectivity that comes with data. It is interesting to note that people trust data much more, indeed, than opinions.
- The four levels should as much as possible use the same data and be asking themselves much the same questions in order to inform decision making for each student, each teacher/classroom, each school, and each district (see the following diagram).

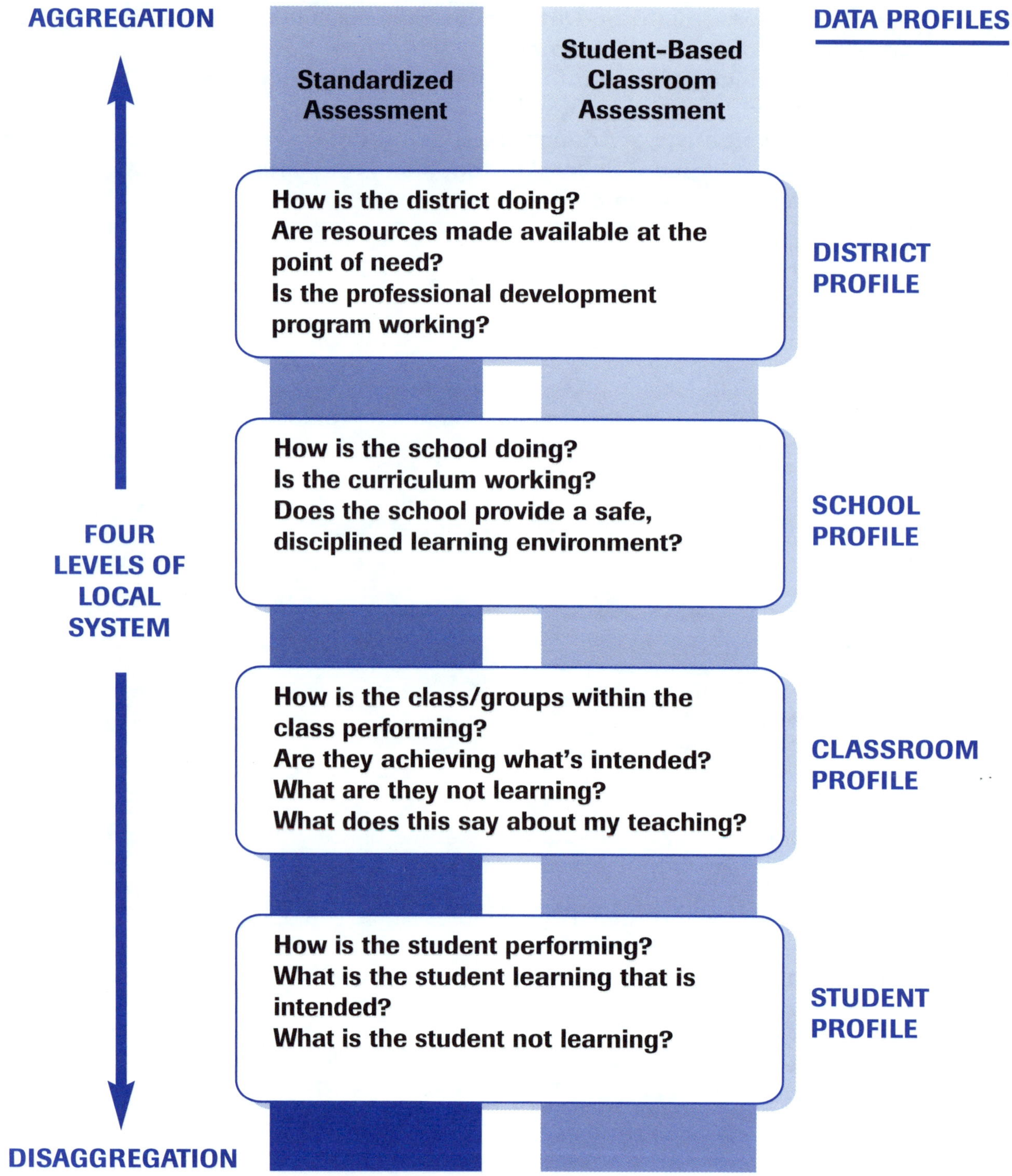
AGGREGATION
Standardized Assessment
Student-Based Classroom Assessment
DATA PROFILES
How is the district doing?
Are resources made available at the point of need?
Is the professional development program working?
DISTRICT PROFILE
How is the school doing?
Is the curriculum working?
Does the school provide a safe, disciplined learning environment?
SCHOOL PROFILE
FOUR LEVELS OF LOCAL SYSTEM
How is the class/groups within the class performing?
Are they achieving what's intended?
What are they not learning?
What does this say about my teaching?
CLASSROOM PROFILE
How is the student performing?
What is the student learning that is intended?
What is the student not learning?
STUDENT PROFILE
DISAGGREGATION

Commendation Two: A stripped-down version of school improvement planning is what is required.

Schmoker's criticisms are well directed. Badly constructed school improvement plans can serve to defeat their own purpose. Stripped-down, "unplugged" (to borrow a term from the music world), lean, and well-focused plans can, however, be most effective—especially if they build in the kind of teamwork envisioned by Schmoker (2003b) in his article. The acid test of all school improvement plans is that they lead to, trigger, and sustain implementation at the classroom/instructional level. Workbooks One: *Conceptualizing a New Path*, Two: *Creating a Process* and Three: *Engaging in Action Research* in this series raise many of the same issues included in Schmoker's article.

One or two goals are the way forward, teamwork is pivotal, and teacher collaboration is the best support mechanism. His arguments, however, shouldn't be allowed to detract from the central importance of rooting cycles of data-driven continuous improvement processes in classrooms, schools, and school districts. Indeed, the NAESP (2001) report, *Essentials for Principals: Data-Based Decision-Making*, recommends the use of the inquiry cycle developed by the Annenberg Institute for School Reform (see the following illustration) that is predicated on the continuous, reflective use of data.

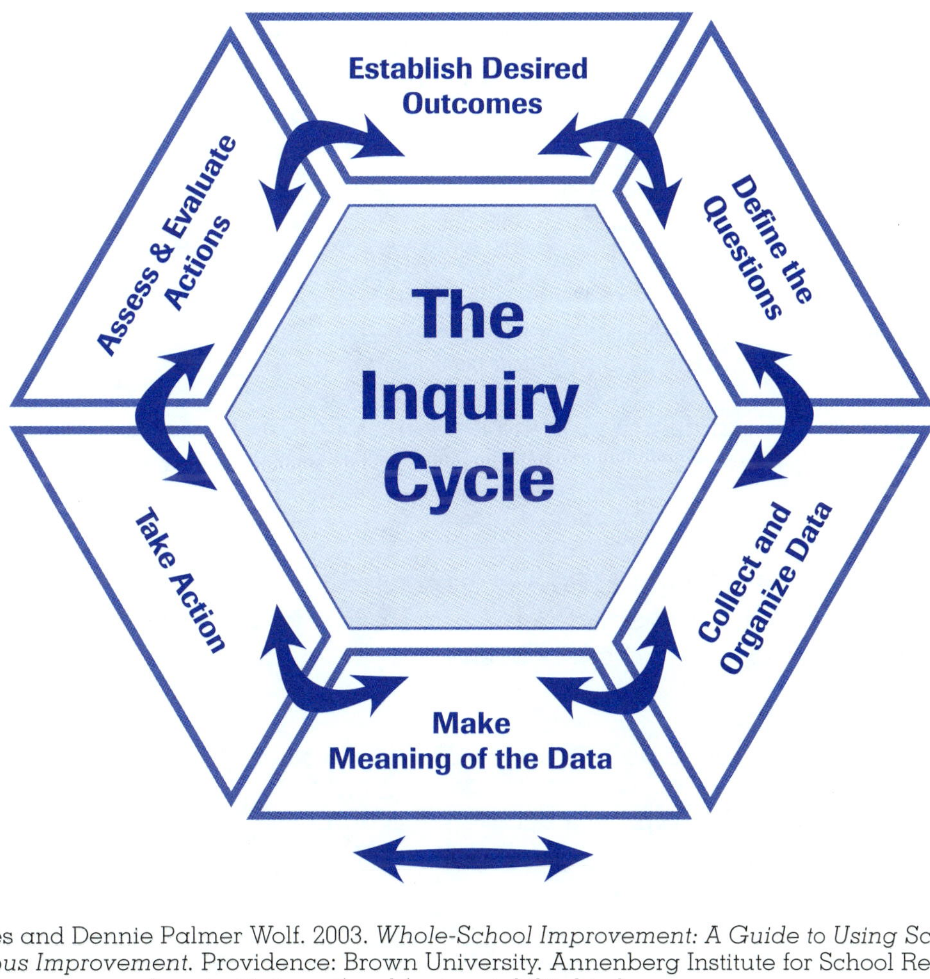

Frank Barnes and Dennie Palmer Wolf. 2003. *Whole-School Improvement: A Guide to Using School Reviews for Continuous Improvement*. Providence: Brown University. Annenberg Institute for School Reform. Available at: www.annenberginstitute.org/work/accountability.html

As in so many other areas (see Workbook Four: *Analyzing and Understanding Data*), successful school improvement planning is a blend of seemingly competing forces. It is both:

- formal and informal
- school-based and team-based
- focused on short-term and long-term, small and large changes
- contractual, yet encouraging of "fleetness-of-foot" and flexibility when it comes to its application
- grounded in internal and external meaning
- for development and accountability

Commendation Three: Allow the data to target our change efforts.

Sanborn (2002) points out that targeted change efforts are so much more likely to hit the mark.

> **If a district does not base continuing educational decisions on careful examination of its data, then fads or good marketing campaigns are more likely to set the agenda. As a result, professional development activities may not be connected to improvement plans (Sanborn, 2002).**

Hirsh (2003) makes much the same point. She reminds us that data-driven decision making is one of the National Staff Development Council's twelve revised standards for staff development. The standard now reads as follows:

> Staff development that improves the learning of all students uses disaggregated student data to determine adult learning priorities, monitor progress, and help sustain continuous improvement.

Wells (2001) reminds us that data-driven decision making helps us move, as Bernhardt (1994) points out, from "random acts of improvement" to "focused acts of improvement." Wells also provides a most useful set of questions to ask of our data to help in the targeting/focusing process:

- How are students doing? How well are they accomplishing standards?
- Are we equitably helping all students to achieve? Who are we serving well? Who not?

- Who needs special help? On what?
- What are the relative strengths and weaknesses of student performance?
- Why are the results as they are?
- Are our special programs working?
- Are specific program components, e.g., professional development, accomplishing their objectives?
- Are new strategies making a difference in student learning?
- What previously hidden challenges do we face?
- Are our day-to-day standards consistent? What do our grades mean?
- Where are our lowest achievers in language arts and math?
- Who are our lowest achievers in language arts and math?
- What factors seem to be contributing to their low achievement?
- What data are easily accessible to teachers?
- What types of data do teachers need in order to make informed changes in their instructional practices?

(Questions amended from Geannie Wells, 2001)

Commendation Four: As our efforts to generate data-driven continuous improvement develop over time, it is important to move from standardization to customization to personalization.

Standardization is the stage when we have large goals and monolithic, all-embracing plans. It is the stage against which Schmoker (2003) has warned us and it is the stage when we think that programs and strategies will work uniformly for all students. We soon find out otherwise. As the plans become more data-driven and more targeted, however, much more customized approaches can be adopted. Disaggregation of data is an important feature at this stage. This is when achievement gaps between various sub-populations of students (see Johnson, 2002) become an important focus. Over time, however, the inescapable lesson emerges: that there is nothing as equitable as a kid-by-kid approach to the data and their learning needs. Personalization of data-use and personalized interventions become the norm.

Deojay and Pennington (2000) have described this crucial work that is mainly carried out under the usual radar screens as follows:

> **Schools are constantly struggling to find ways to meet overall district goals for student performance. Yet too often, they overlook the immediate needs of teachers, whose concerns and energies are focused on the particular students they encounter in the classroom each day.**

The authors present a three-step "problem-solving" framework that encourages teachers to ask questions about the academic performance of their students, gather data that help them pinpoint specific problems that specific students are having, and use these data to modify their classroom practice and evaluate the results. The framework's three steps consist of specifying the current level of student performance, creating an action plan (for each student), and evaluating and communicating progress. It is the kind of problem-solving process that has been applied extensively with special needs students but which, as will be described in Workbook Six: *Exploring and Applying Case Studies*—is being used more and more with individual students generally.

Deojay and Pennington (2000) conclude their article with a powerful description of how the problem-solving process was used to help one particular student—Heather, a fourth grader with writing problems.

Step One: Specifying the Current Level of Student Performance

Heather's progress in writing was causing concerns. By December she seemed stalled and did not appear to be making gains toward the fourth grade curriculum standard ("The student writes clearly and effectively"). Heather was, however, demonstrating appropriate learning behaviors, such as completing classroom and homework assignments within the allotted time, remaining on task during instructional and independent work periods, and participating in cooperative learning group work. To verify Heather's current performance in writing, her teacher used several assessment tools. These included teacher observation, the midterm school writing sample, Heather's portfolio (which revealed that topic, detail, and concluding sentences did not meet criteria), and her record review (which showed that she had received a "below grade level" in written expression for the 3rd grade). In a parent conference, Heather's parents also confirmed that, although she appeared to enjoy the work, writing in her journal at home took Heather a long time.

Step Two: Action Planning

There were three parts to Heather's action plan:

1. A specified, measurable instructional objective.

   Given a story starter and directions to complete the story, Heather was to work independently to write a related story using a topic sentence, at least four supporting sentences, and an ending sentence, with correct punctuation throughout.

2. An instructional intervention.

   The teacher provided a visual prompt (check sheet) for each writing group and explained to the students how the sheet would be used to check if the required elements were included (using a plus sign for the element being present and a minus for the element being missing). The teacher also met with Heather and her parents to explain how to use the check sheet with her journaling at home.

3. Ongoing assessment procedures.

   The instructional intervention was implemented for six weeks. The teacher continued to collect Heather's writing samples and calculated the percentage of criteria met each week.

Step Three: Evaluating and Communicating Progress

The teacher met with Heather weekly to review her work folder (containing her writing samples) and to help her analyze her stories in the light of the expected criteria. The teacher also highlighted the number of plus marks gained on her independent writing assignments by creating a graph so that Heather could see her progress.

The new practice definitely proved effective. Within four weeks, Heather was writing a paragraph according to the specified criteria. She also reported that the check sheet had helped her to remember what to include. In addition, the monthly district-wide writing assessment showed that the whole class had improved in their writing skills.

Commendation Five: Do everything possible for data to impact at the classroom and student learning levels.

As Dennis Sparks says in introducing Deojay and Pennington's paper, the acid test of data analysis is whether it helps teachers make changes in their day-to-day classroom practice in order to improve the learning of each and every Heather.

Reflections
Task 1: Reflecting on the Commentary

Purpose: To reflect on the five cautions and the five commendations.

Grouping: Work on your own and then meet with your Learning Team.

Directions: Your final workbook task is to reflect on the five cautions and the five commendations included in this chapter, first individually and then as a whole team. The essential question at this point is how to be aware of the cautions, while reaping the benefits of the commendations. Use the following chart to guide your individual reflections. Your Learning Team may choose to replicate this chart for the group's shared reflections.

REFLECTIONS ON THE FIVE CAUTIONS AND FIVE COMMENDATIONS	
Caution	**Reflective Notes**
One: School Improvement Plans should release change initiatives, not stifle them.	
Two: Beware of the inadequacies of systemic reform.	
Three: Don't rely solely on the formalized, pre-programmed approaches normally associated with strategic planning.	
Four: Don't undermine the power of people to act as agents of change.	
Five: Don't rely solely on data-based decision making.	
Commendation	**Reflective Notes**
One: All the approaches included in this workbook should be applied with simultaneity and flexibility.	
Two: A stripped-down version of school improvement planning is what is required.	
Three: Allow the data to target our change efforts.	
Four: As our efforts to generate data-driven continuous improvement develop over time, it is important to move from standardization to customization to personalization.	
Five: Do everything possible for data to impact at the classroom and student learning levels.	

POSTSCRIPT

Charles Handy (1989) has argued that most major changes occur as a result of "discontinuous incrementalism." What he meant by this is that for long periods of time small changes are accumulated by accretion; they are assembled incrementally and somewhat separately. Then something happens—a catalyst appears if you will—and a chemical reaction occurs. The accumulated changes react on each other (fusion) and what Handy calls a "flip" occurs which creates something very different from that which existed previously. Henry Mintzberg (1994) refers to this same phenomenon as "emergent" (as opposed to planned) change.

It occurs, he says, when a convergent pattern is formed among a host of informal actions. In the author's estimation, this is exactly what we are now experiencing—the flip at the heart of discontinuous incrementalism, i.e., emergent change. The various pieces—portfolios, computerized management systems, assessments, standards and benchmarks, demands for accountability, and so forth—have all been present but essentially unconnected. Now fusion is occurring and a new formulation is fast appearing to the betterment of school districts, schools, classrooms, and all those Heathers who need the guidance that comes from caring professionals.

ABOUT THE AUTHOR

Peter Holly is the author of the PATHWISE: *Data-Driven School Improvement* series. Having been a teacher, administrator, researcher, and school improvement consultant in the United Kingdom, since 1990 he has worked solely with schools and school districts in the United States. He was one of the lead consultants for Schools for the Twenty-First Century in Washington State, the National Education Association's (NEA) Learning Lab project, and the New Iowa Schools initiative. Currently, he is an independent school improvement consultant working with school systems mainly in the Midwest. In helping school systems become more change-oriented and data-driven, he uses many of the materials to be found in this workbook.

References

American Association of School Administrators (AASA)/Panasonic Foundation. (2002). All Means All, Part 2. *Strategies. For School System Leaders on District-Level Change.* 9(1).

AASA. (2002). The Lingo of Data-Driven Decisions. *The School Administrator Web Edition*. December.

AASA. (2002). Data-Driven Districts. *The School Administrator Web Edition*. December.

AASA. (2002). Providing Data to Your Board. *The School Administrator Web Edition*. December.

AASA. (2002). The Will and the Way of Data Use. *The School Administrator*. December.

Arter, J. and Spandel, V. (1992). Using Portfolios of Student Work in Instruction and Assessment. *Educational Measurement: Issues and Practice. 11*(1).

Association for Supervision and Curriculum Development (ASCD). (1999). New Goals for Teacher Evaluation. *Education Update. 41*(2).

Belanoff, P. and Dickson, M. (eds.) (1991). *Portfolios: Process and Product*. Portsmouth, NH: Boynton/Cook.

Bellamy, G. T., Holly, P. J. and Sinisi, R. V. (1997). *The Cycles of School Improvement*. New Iowa Schools Development Corporation/National Staff Development Council.

Bernhardt, V. L. (1994). *The School Portfolio: A Comprehensive Framework for School Improvement*. Larchmont, NY: Eye On Education.

Bernhardt, V. L. (1998). *Data Analysis for Comprehensive Schoolwide Improvement*. Larchmont, NY: Eye On Education.

Bernhardt, V. L. (2000). Intersections. How "Crossing" Data Can Help You Piece Together a Clearer Picture of Your School. *Journal of Staff Development. 21*(1).

Bernhardt, V. L. (2003). No Schools Left Behind. *Educational Leadership. 60*(5).

Block, P. (2001). *The Answer to How is Yes: Acting on What Matters*. New York: Barrett-Koehler.

Block, P. (2003). The Answer to 'When?' is 'Now.' Interview with Dennis Sparks. *Journal of Staff Development. 24*(2).

Bostingl, J. J. (1992). *Schools of Quality. An Introduction to Total Quality Management in Education*. Alexandria, VA: ASCD.

Brimijoin, K., Marquissee, E. and Tomlinson, C. A. (2003). Using Data to Differentiate Instruction. *Educational Leadership. 60*(5).

Burke, K. (1997). *Designing Professional Portfolios for Change*. Arlington Heights, IL: IRI Skylight Publishing.

Carnahan, D. and Fitzpatrick, M. (2003). Don't Get Buried Under a Mountain of Research. *Journal of Staff Development*. *24*(2).

Cawelti, G. (2003). Lessons from Research that Changed Education. *Educational Leadership*. *60*(5).

Coalition of Essential Schools. (1996). The Tuning Protocol: A Process for Reflection on Teacher and Student Work. *Horace*. November.

Conzemius, A. (2000). Framework. System Builds Change Efforts Beyond Hopes, Hunches, Guesses. *Journal of Staff Development*. *21*(1).

Covey, S. (1989). *The Seven Habits of Highly Effective People*. New York: Simon & Schuster.

Creighton, T. B. (2001). Data Analysis in Administrators' Hands: An Oxymoron? *The School Administrator*. *4*(58).

Cromey, A. (2001). Data Retreats: A Conduit for Change in Schools. In *Using Data for Educational Decision-Making*. The Newsletter of the Comprehensive Center–Region VI, Wisconsin Center for Education Research, The School of Education, University of Wisconsin, Madison.

Danielson, C. (1996). *Enhancing Professional Practice: A Framework for Teaching*. Alexandria, VA: ASCD.

Danielson, C. and Abrutyn, L. (1997). *An Introduction to Using Portfolios in the Classroom*. Alexandria, VA: ASCD.

Danielson, C. and McGreal, T. L. (2000). *Teacher Evaluation to Enhance Professional Practice*. Alexandria, VA: ASCD. Princeton, NJ: Educational Testing Service.

Davies, A., Cameron, C., Politano, C., and Gregory, K. (1992). *Together is Better: Collaborative Assessment, Evaluation and Reporting*. Winnipeg, MB: Peguis.

Dawson, L. (2002). Providing Data to Your Board. *The School Administrator*. December.

Deojay, T. R. and Pennington, L. L. (2000). Reaching Heather. A Framework for Developing Data-based Solutions to Student Learning Problems. *Journal of Staff Development*. *21*(1).

Dietz, M. (1998). *Journals as Frameworks for Change*. Arlington Heights, IL: IRI Skylight Publishing.

Dooley, K. (1997). A Complex Adaptive Systems Model of Organization Change. *Nonlinear Dynamics, Psychology, and Life Science*. *1*(1).

Doyle, D. (2002). Knowledge-Based Decision Making. *The School Administrator. 11*(59).

Duffy, F. M. (2003). I Think, Therefore I am Resistant to Change. *Journal of Staff Development. 24*(1).

Elmore, R. F. (1996). Getting to Scale with Good Educational Practice. *Harvard Educational Review. 66*(1).

Elmore, R. F. (2000). *Building a New Structure for School Leadership.* Washington DC: Albert Shanker Institute.

Elmore, R. F. (2002). Building Capacity to Enhance Learning. A Conversation with Richard Elmore. *Principal Leadership. 2*(5).

Ezarik, M. (2002). Data Digs. *District Administration.* October.

Festinger, L. (1954). *A Theory of Cognitive Dissonance.* Stanford, CA: Stanford.

Feuer, M. J., Towne, L. and Shavelson, R. J. (2002). Scientific Culture and Educational Research. *Educational Researcher. 8*(31).

Fox, D. (2001). Three Kinds of Data for Instructional Decision-Making. In *Using Data for Educational Decision-Making.* The Newsletter of the Comprehensive Center–Region VI, Wisconsin Center for Education Research, The School of Education, University of Wisconsin, Madison.

Fullan, M. (1996). Turning Systemic Thinking on its Head. *Phi Delta Kappan.* February.

Garmston, R. J. (2002). Group Wise. *Journal of Staff Development. 23*(3), 74–75.

Garmston, R. J. and Wellman, B. (1999). *The Adaptive School. A Sourcebook for Developing Collaborative Groups.* Norwood, MA: C. Gordon.

Guskey, T. R. (2003). How Classroom Assessments Improve Learning. *Educational Leadership. 60*(5).

Handy, C. (1989). By Way of Encouragement: The Path to a Better Society. *Royal Society of the Arts (RSA) Journal. CXXXVI*(5377).

Hirsh, S. (2003). Data Tell a School's Full Story. *Results.* December/January.

Holcomb, E. L. (1999). *Getting Excited About Data. How to Combine People, Passion, and Proof.* Thousand Oaks, CA: Corwin Press.

Holly, P. J. (2003). Evidence-Centered Decision Making. In Hessel, K. and Holloway, J. *Case Studies in School Leadership: Keys to a Successful Principalship.* Princeton, NJ: Educational Testing Service.

Holly, P. J. and Lange, M. (2001). *Introduction to the Work of Data Coaches*. Workshop Materials, Dubuque CSD, Iowa.

Holly, P. J. and Lange, M. (2002). *Practical Purposes of the School Profile*. Workshop Materials, Dubuque CSD, Iowa.

Hunter, M. C. (1982). *Mastery Teaching*. Thousand Oaks, CA: Corwin Press.

Johnson, Ruth S. (2002). *Using Data to Close the Achievement Gap*. Thousand Oaks, CA: Corwin Press.

Johnson, D. W. and Johnson, F. P. (2000). *Joining Together. Group Theory and Group Skills*. Boston: Allyn and Bacon.

Keefe, J. W. and Jenkins, J. M. (2002). Personalized Instruction. *Phi Delta Kappan*. *83*(6).

Killion, J. (2003). Use These Six Keys to Open Doors to Literacy. *Journal of Staff Development*. *24*(2).

Killion, J. and Bellamy, G. T. (2000). On the Job. The Position of Data Analyst Focuses on School Improvement Efforts. *Journal of Staff Development*. *21*(1).

Klempen, R. (2003). Reinventing Decision Making. *The School Administrator*. *2*(60).

LaBoskey, V. K. (2000). Portfolios Here, Portfolios There…Searching for the Essence of 'Educational Portfolios'. *Phi Delta Kappan*. *81*(8).

Lafee, S. (2002). Data-Driven Districts. *The School Administrator*. *11*(59).

Langer, G. S. (1996). Teacher Portfolios: Tools for Improving Teaching and Learning. *Education Update*. December.

Linn, R., Baker, E. and Betebenner, D. (2002). Accountability Systems: Implications of Requirements of the No Child Left Behind Act of 2001. *Educational Researcher*. *31*(6).

Martin-Kniep, G. (1999). Teacher Portfolios for Successful Evaluations. *Education Update*. *41*(2).

Marzano, R. J. (2000). *Transforming Classroom Grading*. Alexandria, VA: ASCD.

Marzano, R. J. (2003). Using Data: Two Wrongs and a Right. *Educational Leadership*. *60*(5).

McGreal, T. (1996). On a New Direction for Teacher Evaluation. A Conversation with Ron Brandt. *Educational Leadership*. March.

McTighe, J. and Ferrara, S. (1998). *Assessing Learning in the Classroom*. Washington, DC: National Education Association (NEA).

Mintzberg, H. (1994). The Fall and Rise of Strategic Planning. *Harvard Business Review*. January–February.

Morgan, E. (2001). The Benefits of Data Management in the Classroom. In *Using Data for Educational Decision-Making*. The Newsletter of the Comprehensive Center–Region VI, Wisconsin Center for Education Research, The School of Education, University of Wisconsin, Madison.

National Association of Elementary School Principals (NAESP). (2001). *Essentials for Principals: Data-Based Decision-Making*. Arlington, VA: Educational Research Service.

NEA. (1993). *Student Portfolios*. Washington, DC: NEA Professional Library.

North Central Association Commission on Schools (NCA). (2000). *Developing the School Profile. A Handbook for Schools*. Tempe, AZ: NCA.

North Central Regional Educational Laboratory (NCREL). (2001). *Data Retreats*. Aurora, IL: NCREL.

Noyce, P., Perda, D. and Traver, R. (2000). Creating Data-Driven Schools. *Educational Leadership*. February.

Olson, L. (2002). Data-Driven: An Occasional Series. *Education Week on the Web*, 6/12/2002.

Peck, S. (1987). *The Different Drum: Community Making and Peace*. New York: Simon & Schuster.

Peters, T. (1987). *Thriving on Chaos*. New York: Alfred A. Knopf.

PQ Systems. (1996). *Pocket Tools for Education*. Miamisburg, OH.

Reeves, D. (2001). Standards Make a Difference: The Influence of Standards on Classroom Assessment. *NASSP Bulletin, Special Edition: Standards and Assessment Practices*. *85*(621).

Resnick, L. B. and Resnick, D. P. (1992). Assessing the Thinking Curriculum: New Tools for Educational Reform. In Gifford, B. R. and O'Connor, M. C. (eds.), *Changing Assessments: Alternative Views of Aptitude, Achievement and Instruction*. Boston: Kluwer Academic Press.

Richardson, J. (2002). Reach for the Stars. Individual Learning Plans Allow Teachers to Take Charge of Their Own Learning. *Tools for Schools*. February/March.

Richardson, J. (2003). The Secrets of 'Can-Do' Schools. *Results*. February.

Rudner, L. M. and Boston, C. (2003). Data Warehousing: Beyond Disaggregation. *Educational Leadership*. *60*(5).

Sanborn, J. (2002). Targeted Training. *The School Administrator*. *11*(59).

Schmoker, M. (2003). First Things First: Demystifying Data Analysis. *Educational Leadership*. *60*(5).

Schmoker, M. (2003b). Planning For Failure? *Education Week*. 2/12/03.

Senge, P. (1990). *The Fifth Discipline*. New York: Doubleday.

Slavin, R. (2003). A Reader's Guide to Scientifically Based Research. *Educational Leadership*. *60*(5).

Spandel, V. and Culham, R. (1995). *Putting Portfolio Stories to Work*. Portland, OR: Northwest Regional Educational Laboratory.

Stiggins, R. J. (1997). *Student-Centered Classroom Assessment*. Second Edition. Upper Saddle River, NJ: Merrill.

Stiggins, R. J. (1998). Speech on *Student-Centered Classroom Assessment*. Area Education Agency 5, Fort Dodge, Iowa.

Stiggins, R. J. (guest ed.). (2001). Standards and Assessment Practices. *NASSP Bulletin, Special Section*. *85*(621).

Streifer, P. A. (2001). The 'Drill Down' Process. *The School Administrator*. *4*(58).

Streifer, P.A. and Kisiel, R. (2002). *Using Data to Make Better Educational Decisions*. Arlington, VA: American Association of School Administrators (AASA).

Thompson, S. (2003). Creating a High-Performance System. *Phi Delta Kappan*. *84*(7).

Wells, G. (2001). *Data Driven Decision Making*. AASA Center for Accountability Solutions (CAS), Workshop Presentation.

Winograd, P. and Webb, K. S. (1994). Impact on Curriculum and Instruction. In Guskey, T. R. (ed.), *High Stakes Performance Assessment: Perspectives on Kentucky's Educational Reform*. Thousand Oaks, CA: Corwin Press.

Wolf, D. P. (2002). When Raising Isn't Rising. *The School Administrator*. *11*(59).

Wolf, K. (1996). Developing an Effective Teaching Portfolio. *Educational Leadership*. March.

Wolf, K., Lichenstein, G. and Stevenson, C. (1997). Using Teaching Portfolios in Teacher Evaluation. In Stronge, J. (ed.), *Teacher Assessment and Evaluation: A Guide for Research and Practice*. Thousand Oaks, CA: Corwin Press.

Yeagley, R. (2001). Data in Your Hands. *The School Administrator*. *4*(58).

Yeagley, R. (2002). A Forum for Becoming Data Savvy. *The School Administrator Web Edition*. December.

Notes

Appendix A
A Framework for Teaching

Domain 1
PLANNING AND PREPARATION

1a: Demonstrating Knowledge of Content and Pedagogy

Knowledge of content
Knowledge of prerequisite relationships
Knowledge of content-related pedagogy

1b: Demonstrating Knowledge of Students

Knowledge of characteristics of age group
Knowledge of students' varied approaches to learning
Knowledge of students' skills and knowledge
Knowledge of students' interests and cultural heritage

1c: Selecting Instructional Goals

Value
Clarity
Suitability for diverse students
Balance

1d: Demonstrating Knowledge of Resources

Resources for teaching
Resources for students

1e: Designing Coherent Instruction

Learning activities
Instructional materials and resources
Instructional groups
Lesson and unit structure

1f: Assessing Student Learning

Congruence with instructional goals
Criteria and standards
Use for planning

Domain 2
THE CLASSROOM ENVIRONMENT

2a: Creating an Environment of Respect and Rapport

Teacher interaction with students
Student interaction

2b: Establishing a Culture for Learning

Importance of content
Student pride in work
Expectations for learning and achievement

2c: Managing Classroom Procedures

Management of instructional groups
Management of transitions
Management of materials and supplies
Performance of noninstructional duties
Supervision of volunteers and paraprofessionals

2d: Managing Student Behavior

Expectations
Monitoring of student behavior
Response to student misbehavior

2e: Organizing Physical Space

Safety and arrangement of furniture
Accessibility to learning and use of physical resources

Source: *Enhancing Professional Practice: A Framework for Teaching* by Charlotte Danielson (1996).

Domain 3
INSTRUCTION

3a: Communicating Clearly and Accurately

Directions and procedures
Oral and written language

3b: Using Questioning and Discussion Techniques

Quality of questions
Discussion techniques
Student participation

3c: Engaging Students in Learning

Representation of content
Activities and assignments
Grouping of students
Instructional materials and resources
Structure and pacing

3d: Providing Feedback to Students

Quality: accurate, substantive, constructive, and specific
Timeliness

3e: Demonstrating Flexibility and Responsiveness

Lesson adjustment
Response to students
Persistence

Domain 4
PROFESSIONAL RESPONSIBILITIES

4a: Reflecting on Teaching

Accuracy
Use in future teaching

4b: Maintaining Accurate Records

Student completion of assignments
Student progress in learning
Noninstructional records

4c: Communicating with Families

Information about the instructional program
Information about individual students
Engagement of families in the instructional program

4d: Contributing to the School and District

Relationships with colleagues
Service to the school
Participation in school and district projects

4e: Growing and Developing Professionally

Enhancement of content knowledge and pedagogical skill
Service to the profession

4f: Showing Professionalism

Service to students
Advocacy
Decision making

Appendix B: Linking a Framework for Teaching With State Teaching Standards

Domain	Iowa Teaching Standard	Data to Collect for Evidence
Domain 1: Planning and Preparation • Demonstrating Knowledge of Content and Pedagogy • Demonstrating Knowledge of Students • Selecting Instructional Goals • Demonstrating Knowledge of Resources • Designing Coherent Instruction • Assessing Student Learning	**Iowa Teaching Standards** #1. Demonstrates ability to enhance academic performance and support for implementation of the school district's student achievement goals. #2. Demonstrates competence in content knowledge appropriate to the teaching position. #3. Demonstrates competence in planning and preparing for instruction. #5. Uses a variety of methods to monitor student learning.	**Data to collect to provide evidence of Domain 1** • Documentation – Standards and benchmarks/grade level expectations and their use in instructional planning – Instructional plans for single lessons – Three-week unit plans – Planned assessment activities and procedures – Student records/spreadsheets containing learning results, demographic information, and attempted interventions – Standardized test item analysis – Sample IEPs/individual learning plans – Knowledge of students and resources sheet • Interviews: demonstrates the ability to explain instructional goals relative to – District curriculum guidelines – State frameworks – Coherent standards – Appropriateness for students
Domain 2: The Classroom Environment • Creating an Environment of Respect and Rapport • Establishing a Culture for Learning • Managing Classroom Procedures • Managing Student Behavior • Organizing Physical Space	**Iowa Teaching Standards** #6. Demonstrates competence in classroom management.	**Data to collect to provide evidence of Domain 2** • Observation records and reports • Student surveys, e.g., student resiliency surveys • Student interviews and feedback • "Walkabout" studies • Self-assessments • Agreed upon statements after post-observation conferences (including personal goals) • Videotapes, photographs, and audiotapes • Climate/perception/attitude surveys • Demographic analysis • Student and teacher logs and journals

<table>
<tr><th>Domain</th><th>Iowa Teaching Standard</th><th>Data to Collect for Evidence</th></tr>
<tr>
<td>Domain 3: Instruction
• Communicating Clearly and Accurately
• Using Questioning and Discussion Techniques
• Engaging Students in Learning
• Providing Feedback to Students
• Demonstrating Flexibility and Responsiveness</td>
<td>Iowa Teaching Standards
#4. Uses strategies to deliver instruction that meets the multiple learning needs of students.
#5. Uses a variety of methods to monitor student learning.</td>
<td>Data to collect to provide evidence of Domain 3
• Reflective logs and journals; reflection sheets
• Self-assessments
• Student feedback, surveys, and interviews
• Norm-referenced and criterion-referenced tests
• "Up-close" data, e.g., reading probes
• Peer observations
• "Walkabout" studies
• Samples of student work
• Audio-visual recordings
• Flanders Interaction Analysis Categories (FIAC)
• Instructional artifact sheet
• Instructional plans and records
• Sample IEPs/individual learning plans</td>
</tr>
<tr>
<td>Domain 4: Professional Responsibilities
• Reflecting on Teaching
• Maintaining Accurate Records
• Communicating with Families
• Contributing to the School and District
• Growing and Developing Professionally
• Showing Professionalism</td>
<td>Iowa Teaching Standards
#7. Engages in professional growth.
#8. Fulfills professional responsibilities established by the school district.</td>
<td>Data to collect to provide evidence of Domain 4
• Documentation (in a Teacher Portfolio)
– Family Contact Log
– School and District Contribution Log
– Professional Contribution Log
– Professional Development Log
– Action research reports
– Reflective journals
– Sample letters, news sheets, and so forth
– Instructional records/sample lesson plans
– Grade book/assessment sheets/parent reports
– Administrator letters of reference/testimonials
– Record of in-service activities/class and conference attendance records
– Professional Growth Plan
– Anecdotal records</td>
</tr>
</table>

Appendix C: National Staff Development Council Worksheets

WORKSHEET 1: DATA COLLECTION WORKSHEET

Reflection Questions

What do I need to do to keep developing professionally?

How could I grow professionally to meet the needs of my students?

If I have three to five years to complete my goals, how can I develop a plan that enables me to have a focused, sustained effort over this period of time?

How could I engage in learning within my school setting?

How will I identify goals that are critical to my professional growth and to student learning?

How could I further the district and building goals?

How could my colleagues participate in my professional growth?

Source: The tools on these pages have been adapted from work done by the Eisenhower National Clearinghouse with additional suggestions from the South Western City Schools, and the Ohio Education Association.

WHAT DATA DID YOU EXAMINE? *Be specific about the source of your data.*

WHAT DOES THIS SUGGEST?

What strengths do you see in your practice?

What areas for improvement can you identify?

What other questions does it suggest for you?

What other information do you need to collect?

WHAT DATA DID YOU EXAMINE? *Be specific about the source of your data.*

WHAT DOES THIS SUGGEST?

What strengths do you see in your practice?

What areas for improvement can you identify?

What other questions does it suggest for you?

What other information do you need to collect?

WORKSHEET 2: SUMMARIZE YOUR INFORMATION

Reflection Questions

What experiences have shaped me as an educator?

What do others say about my strengths and my weaknesses as an educator and a colleague?

In what situations do I feel most or least competent?

What attracts me to a learning experience? Why?

What makes me want to avoid a learning experience? Why?

What strengths and weaknesses have I discovered by reflecting on what I like and what I like to avoid?

Based on the data-collection worksheet, create three or four summary statements that you want to develop into professional development goals.

The summary statements should be descriptions of what you learned from examining the data. They should not attempt to propose a solution or a course of action.

STATEMENT 1:

____

____

____

____

____

____

STATEMENT 2:

____

____

____

____

____

____

STATEMENT 3:

____

____

____

____

____

____

STATEMENT 4:

____

____

____

____

____

____

WORKSHEET 3: INDIVIDUAL LEARNING PLAN

Reflection Questions

How will I change as a result of participating in this activity?

Will this activity foster collegiality?

How can I link this activity to the work of colleagues?

How can my learning activity benefit my colleagues?

Who can I call upon for feedback?

What evidence of my learning will I produce?

What will I observe, count, or measure to determine whether the changes in practice stemming from this activity have improved student learning?

What will be the first indication of student learning that I can expect to see?

How long will it be before improvement can be measured?

Your plan will consist of several goals. Use this sheet to create a plan for a single goal that is part of your larger plan.

1. **GOALS.** What is your goal and how does it relate to student needs and building or district goals?

____

____

____

Example: Improve student performance on science proficiency tests, based on the number of students who must take the test more than once and the district goal that 90% of students should pass the test the first time they take it.

2. **OBJECTIVES.** What specific objectives do you expect to accomplish?

____

____

____

Example: Within the next two years, my classroom practice will enable 90% of my students to pass the science proficiency test the first time they take it.

3. **POTENTIAL ACTIVITIES.** What specific activities will you undertake that are directly related to these objectives?

____

____

____

Example: Take classes and/or workshops to improve my ability to implement inquiry-based learning in my classroom; collaborate with or seek mentoring from other teachers who use inquiry learning.

4. **RELEVANCE.** How is the scope of the plan relevant to the subject area you teach, your students, your building/district goals, and quality educational practice?

____

____

____

Example: Inquiry is an important and widely acknowledged method for effectively teaching science and will enable me to increase my students' performance on proficiency tests.

5. **EVALUATION CRITERIA.** What are the criteria for determining the success of your objectives? When and how will you adjust your plan if needed?

____

____

____

Example: In two years, 90% of my students will pass the science proficiency test; if after one year, they are not making progress, I will review and adjust my strategy.

WORKSHEET 4: INDIVIDUAL GOALS FOR PROFESSIONAL DEVELOPMENT

Reflection Questions

How does this learning activity link to what I already know?

Why am I considering this particular activity?

What resources will I request for this activity?

What resources are essential for this activity?

How can they be obtained?

What resources can I do without if necessary?

In what way will this learning activity deepen my understanding of a specific subject area or subject-specific teaching method?

How does this activity relate to other learning activities I intend to pursue?

How comfortable will I be engaging in this activity?

What will be the easiest and most difficult parts of this activity?

Use one sheet for each goal that you identify.

EXAMPLES OF LEARNING GOALS

I will:

- Know and apply strategies for extending student thinking.
- Become knowledgeable about diverse cultures and apply new learning to the classroom.
- Deepen my understanding of quality work attributes; design and implement quality work for students.
- Read widely in the area of collegial learning; create opportunities for collegial learning among the staff.
- Research school reform and leadership literature related to the roll of the principal in school improvement; design strategies related to administrative work.

GOAL

1. I will: ____________________
2. In what area: ____________________
3. And then: ____________________

BASIS FOR YOUR GOAL

How does your goal link to your individual needs? What data did you use to identify your needs?

How does your goal link to your building goals?

How does your goal link to the district's improvement plan?

How does your goal link to improving student achievement?

EVIDENCE OF ACCOMPLISHMENT

What evidence will you submit to show what you have accomplished?

When will you review your plan and make adjustments?

These materials are being sponsored by the Teaching and Learning Division of Educational Testing Service (ETS), a not for profit organization. One of the division's goals is to serve teachers' professional development needs by providing products and services that identify, assess, and advance good teaching from initial preparation through advanced practice.

ETS®

Our mission is to help advance quality and equity in education by providing fair and valid assessments, research and related services. Our products and services measure knowledge and skills, promote learning and performance, and support education and professional development for all people worldwide.

We welcome your comments and feedback.

E-mail address: professionaldevelopment@ets.org

Professional Development Group
Teaching and Learning Division
Educational Testing Service, MS 18-D
Princeton, New Jersey 08541